THE **G**LOBE **R**EADER'S **C**OLLECTION

STORIES OF
ADVENTURE AND
SURVIVAL

GLOBE FEARON EDUCATIONAL PUBLISHER
A Division of Simon & Schuster
Upper Saddle River, New Jersey

Executive Editor: Barbara Levadi
Senior Editor: Bernice Golden
Editors: Helene Avraham, Laura Baselice, Robert McIlwaine
Product Development: PubWorks, Inc.
Production Manager: Penny Gibson
Senior Production Editor: Linda Greenberg
Production Editor: Walt Niedner
Marketing Manager: Sandra Hutchison
Electronic Page Production: The Wheetley Company, Inc.
Cover Design: The Wheetley Company, Inc.
Cover Art: Frederick Edwin Church's *Twilight in the Wilderness*, Cleveland Museum of Art, Ohio; Bridgeman Art Library, London; SuperStock, Inc.
Illustrations: Krystyna Stasiak

Printed in the United States of America
 2 3 4 5 6 7 8 9 10 99 98 97

ISBN: 0-8359-1380-5

GLOBE FEARON EDUCATIONAL PUBLISHER
A Division of Simon & Schuster
Upper Saddle River, New Jersey

TABLE OF CONTENTS

Personal Survival

READING STORIES OF ADVENTURE AND SURVIVAL

You can't predict what will happen in life. After all, life can be an adventure. No one knows what the future will bring. Of course, you can try and make plans. You can make a date to visit a friend or to go and see a movie. Looking forward to these things can be fun. However, things do not always go according to plan. A rainy day or a flat tire can cancel your plans or bring them to an end.

Then there are adventures that you probably never want to have. Have you ever dreamed of being trapped in a fire or threatened by a flood? These are real-life adventures that you surely could live without. However, if one of them happened to you, would you know what to do to survive?

Reading stories about survival is itself an exciting adventure. Some of these stories, such as "Riding Out the Storm," are meant to teach a lesson in life. Others, such as "Coming Through the Fire," are clearly written as exciting adventures. All of them depend upon suspense for their excitement. What is suspense? Suspense is a feeling of growing tension, curiosity, and sometimes fear, felt by the reader. Be sure to look for the various ways that the writers of these stories create suspense. Are clues given to some dreaded event about to happen? Or are people trying to survive some event that is already taking place?

As you read adventure and survival stories, you share the terror of people whose lives are in danger. You also share their relief when they are brought to safety. Most of the stories in this book are based on events that actually happened. The rest of the stories certainly could happen–and they could happen to you!

Stories of Adventure and Survival has five units. In the first, "A Helping Hand," you will read about people who probably would have died if it had not been for the bravery of others. You will read about people diving into the sea, hiking through a jungle, or battling a hurricane to save someone they care about.

The titles of the next three units are "Trial by Fire," "Waves of Panic," and "Freezing Fears." Can you guess what the stories in each of these units are about? They all have something in common. They all show the awesome fury of nature. Sometimes, nature cannot be tamed. But, sometimes, we can survive it.

Imagine yourself in a life-threatening situation. Now, imagine that you are alone. You have only yourself to depend on. You must rely on your strength and your intelligence and—most of all—your will to live. Will you make it? Read the last unit, "Personal Survival," to see how others handled their life-and-death struggles.

Unit 1

A Helping Hand

WE JUST KEPT WALKING

Krista Kanenwisher

If you found yourself adrift in a life raft on the open sea, do you think you'd survive? In the following story, you'll see how some WWI sailors handled this problem.

The leader of the shipwrecked group is Arthur Murphy Jones. He found strength in some memories about his Native American heritage. His grandmother had told him about the famous Trail of Tears which occurred around 150 years ago. In that tragic incident, many Native Americans were forced to leave their homelands to march west on a deadly trail. About 4,000 Cherokee died on the 116-day march to Oklahoma in bitter cold. Remembering how his family had faced that challenge helped Art to overcome this one.

VOCABULARY WORDS

scanning (SKAN-ihng) looking at closely, searching
❖ Our radar was *scanning* the sky for signs of enemy planes.

angular (AN-gyoo-luhr) with sharp facial features
❖ Mr. Lockhart was tall, thin, and *angular*.

devastating (DEHV-uhs-tayt-ihng) destructive
❖ Much property was recently destroyed in the Midwest by *devastating* floods.

winced (WIHNSD) pulled back and made a face due to fear or embarrassment
❖ I *winced* when Mom mentioned my science grades.

dehydration (dee-hy-DRAY-shuhn) loss of water from body tissues
❖ After even a few hours in the desert, you run the risk of *dehydration*.

KEY WORDS

rations (RASH-uhnz) food supply for soldiers
❖ After their *rations* were gone, the men in the lifeboat tried to catch fish to eat.

Tecumseh (tih-KUM-suh) small town in Oklahoma
❖ The town of *Tecumseh* is named after a Shawnee chief.

Trail of Tears route followed in 1838 by the Cherokee and other Native Americans on their forced march from Georgia, Tennessee, and Florida to Oklahoma
❖ Thousands of Native Americans died on the *Trail of Tears*.

"**M**y name is Arthur Murphy Jones. My name is Arthur Murphy Jones. My name . . ." Art kept murmuring his name, trying to stay conscious as the heat of the sun reflected off the ocean. Eleven men, who had scarcely known each other before the submarine assignment, were now shipwrecked together, floating in a Navy life raft.

"Are you OK?" the men asked each other anxiously when they first got into the raft.

"What do we do now?" some of them asked.

"Well," answered the most experienced sailor, "it's just a waiting game now."

The ocean waves tossed the raft furiously. The grim reality of being shipwrecked seemed to be anchored in their stomachs instead of their brains. Their submarine was the first to be sunk in World War I.

"Pass those binoculars over here, Art," Hank said.

The men had only one pair of binoculars. Each man took his turn scanning the horizon for a rescue ship. They watched continuously, as long as there was any reflection from the sun.

"Won't be long now," one of the men kept saying.

"Yeah," answered another, "we'll be eating apple pie with ice cream before you know it."

"I'll take a steak myself," piped up the youngest sailor and everyone laughed.

They had been on the overcrowded raft for more than a week now. Their sea rations had run out several days before, and their supply of drinking water was nearly gone. The guys on the raft had talked about every conceivable topic. Now it was time to start forming a game plan. Art insisted that they develop a plan and use it until there was no one left to do the work.

3

At first, the men had tried to use the paddles to direct the raft. But they argued about their location. They sent up flares the first two nights, but decided that they might attract enemy ships. There had been no time to send a distress signal.

They tried making masts and sails. They determined a course that they should try to take. And they shortened the time that each man would use the binoculars. They were hoping that the men would be more alert if they were given shorter stretches of time to be on watch.

"My name is Arthur Murphy Jones. I am Arthur . . . take me home." The gentle rocking of the raft helped Arthur drift into a deep sleep and the healing nourishment of a dream. He was swept away to the tree-lined streets of Tecumseh, Oklahoma where he lived. He was walking across the lawn of his grandmother's old home. He could feel a breeze on his cheek. He could hear it as it fluttered the leaves on the cottonwood trees. His grandmother sat in her rocking chair on the front porch. Her Cherokee heritage was etched in her face. Long braids were wrapped in a circle and pinned to the back of her head. Her shoulders were covered by her purple shawl, and her house dress was unusually long. She still wore the traditional moccasins. Her thin, angular body gave an impression of height, but when she stood, she was not even five feet tall. Her elderly face held a slight smile, as if she knew that her grandson could see her.

Arthur looked around the place of his childhood. He could smell the pear trees and the lilacs that were in full bloom. He moved to the porch step and watched his grandmother as she rocked. Selma was a wonder to him. She was emotionally and spiritually stronger than any other human being he had ever known.

When he was a little boy, she told him how her family had walked the Trail of Tears. For hundreds of years, her Cherokee ancestors had lived in small villages along the rivers and streams of Tennessee and Georgia. In order to make room for white settlers, President Andrew Jackson ordered soldiers to force the Cherokee from their homeland. Beginning in 1838 and lasting many cold winter months, more than 16,000 Cherokee and members of four other tribes—the Choctaw, Chickasaw, Creek, and Seminole—marched west. It was a death march. Men, women, and children were pushed cruelly forward by soldiers. Many died along the way. But Selma's mother was determined to keep her family together. She had figured out the system that the army used to divide the families. She had placed her children, nieces, and nephews in different huts so that the numbering system would bring them back together.

The dream continued. . . . Rising from her rocking chair, Selma left the porch of the old house and walked down the hill towards the family cemetery. From her lips, Arthur could hear the low hum of a Cherokee lullaby. The first year following the death march had been a terrible one for the Cherokee in Oklahoma. Those families who had not been allowed to bring crop seeds or who were not fortunate enough to be allotted lands with streams or creeks were desperate for food. Between the march and the first winter, almost one in four Cherokee lives were lost.

Grandmother moved slowly past each of the graves: Harjo, Tuscany, Chicola, Chicote, Tustenuggee. She moved past his cousins' graves: Thomas, John, and Peter. His cousins had died from childhood diseases. Each new wave of settlers to the territories brought another disease. Smallpox, chicken pox, polio, and measles were among the most devastating illnesses. And with each new disease, many of the Cherokee children were lost. Selma described to Arthur how hard the march had been. She told him how tired the people were and how sad they were when they were not allowed to stop and bury their dead. Arthur had asked her, "Well, what did our people do then?" She answered, "They just kept walking, Arthur." Each time that she told more about the march, he would ask her, "What then?" And she would always answer, "They just kept walking."

Arthur winced in his sleep, as he dreamed of his grandmother moving past his mother's grave. He had been twelve when she died. He remembered that his grandmother used to wipe away his tears and whisper, "We'll just keep walking, Arthur."

Art was awakened by men yelling. They were trying to pull Hank Williams from the water. Arthur wondered whether he had fallen off the raft or whether he had simply given up. "Pull him in! He's too weak to swim! Come on, Hank, swim! You've gotta swim!"

Arthur dove into the cold Atlantic water. The men were reaching for him. "Art, you can't get him! Come on back!" They were all shouting. Finally, Hank looked up at the crew. He looked at Art thrashing through the water, and he began to swim. Art was with him, swimming and screaming. "Come on, Hank! Swim!" The two of them struggled to the raft. Finally, Arthur pushed Hank aboard.

As Hank and Art sat shivering on board the raft, the weather began to improve. The winds that had been tossing them about were now cooperating with their hand-made sails. Art encouraged the men to make some shade for the sailors who were in the most danger of dying from dehydration.

6

That day and night passed uneventfully. Early on the morning of the tenth day, Hank heard a plane. Flying low over the raft, the plane dipped its wings back and forth. It seemed to be a signal acknowledging their situation. The men knew that their rescue was close at hand. Six hours later, a U.S. Navy warship came into view.

The men waited for the ship to send out small lifeboats towards the raft. Art smiled as the men tried to wash their faces, button up their shirts, or straighten up their clothing as well as they could.

Since there had been no officer aboard, the men had appointed Art as their leader. He now stood in salute, as the small lifeboats began to pull up beside the raft. A worried captain saluted the men. Looking at Art, he asked, "How have you managed to survive, sailor?" Tearfully, Art replied, "We just kept walking, sir."

READING FOR UNDERSTANDING

The following paragraph summarizes the story. Decide which of the words below the paragraph best fits in each blank. Write your answers on a separate sheet of paper.

For many cold winter months, the Cherokee and the members of four other Native American **(1)**_____ were forced to march west. Selma's mother struggled to keep her family together, but many of the marchers **(2)**_____. Selma showed Arthur the family graves in the **(3)**_____. He asked her how people were able to endure such hardships. She answered, "They just kept **(4)**_____, Arthur." When Art woke up, he found the men trying to pull Hank Williams from the water. Art dove in and managed to **(5)**_____ Hank. On the morning of the **(6)**_____ day, the men finally heard a **(7)**_____. They were rescued by lifeboats sent out by a U.S. Navy warship. The worried **(8)**_____ asked Art how the men had managed to survive. "We just kept walking, sir," Art replied.

Words: *tribes, tenth, captain, walking, died, cemetery, plane, rescue*

RESPONDING TO THE STORY

When Art needed a source of strength and inspiration, he remembered the stories that his grandmother had told him when he was a child. What do you think about when you need strength? Write about it in a paragraph.

REVIEWING VOCABULARY

1. A *devastating* storm is one that **(a)** blows in from the northeast **(b)** affects a huge area **(c)** causes very serious damage.

2. An *angular* person has **(a)** a scheming mind **(b)** sharp facial features **(c)** a good appetite.

3. If your body is suffering from *dehydration*, you need **(a)** heat **(b)** water **(c)** an operation.

4. When Mary *winced* at the remark, she seemed to **(a)** react angrily **(b)** agree completely **(c)** pull back and make a face.

5. If a person is *scanning* the horizon, he or she is probably **(a)** searching for something **(b)** testing a short-wave radio **(c)** trying to calculate the moment of sunset.

THINKING CRITICALLY

1. The men shouted to Art to get back to the raft, yet he risked his life to save Hank. Why do you think Art did this?

2. Why do you think the men on the raft appointed Art as their leader?

3. How do you think Art's grandmother might have reacted to the news of her grandson's wartime experience? Discuss what she might have said to him in response to the news.

4. In what ways were Selma's stories about the past a lesson for Art on how to survive extreme hardship?

5. What do you think of Art's ancestors' response to the Trail of Tears? Do you think they could they have behaved differently? Would it have helped?

THE BABY IN THE WELL

Jeffrey Cooper

Several years ago in Texas, a baby fell down a well shaft. As people struggled to save her, the whole world held its breath. Television and radio stations and newspapers around the world covered the story of Baby Jessica. In cities and towns throughout the globe, her fate was discussed at work, at school, and in homes.

What was there about this news story that made it of interest to so many people? Why did they care so much about a baby they didn't even know?

As you read about Baby Jessica, pay attention to your own reactions. Try to figure out what makes "The Baby in the Well" such a compelling story.

VOCABULARY WORDS

shaft (SHAFT) long, narrow opening dug into the earth
❖ To reach oil, the workers had to drill a deep *shaft* into the ground.

welling (WEHL-lihng) pouring forth; gushing
❖ The tears were *welling* up in my eyes, as I learned the sad news.

site (SYT) specific place
❖ The *site* for the monument was the place where the battle had been fought.

grueling (GROO-uhl-ihng) difficult and exhausting
❖ Cleaning a dirty oven can be *grueling* work.

ordeal (awr-DEEL) painful experience
❖ Getting home through the ice and snow proved to be an *ordeal*.

paramedic (PAR-uh-mehd-ihk) emergency medical worker
❖ The *paramedic* rushed to help the injured people.

blurted (BLERT-uhd) said suddenly without thinking
❖ He *blurted* out the truth to everyone in the court-room.

swaddled (SWAHD-uhld) wrapped in cloth
❖ We *swaddled* the baby in an old blanket to keep her warm.

plaque (PLAK) thin piece of wood or metal with lettering on it
❖ According to the *plaque* on the building, a famous poet had once lived there.

Looking for excitement? I suggest you look just about anywhere but here. Our sleepy little town of Midland, Texas, is not exactly a tourist attraction. Nothing much happens here. About the most exciting thing is the annual Founders' Day parade. Usually, even that little stroll down Main Street is pretty dull. I've been editing Midland's weekly newspaper for over twenty years now. There have been plenty of times when I was hard-pressed to come up with enough local news to fill the front page, much less the rest of the paper.

Then came that one eventful week in the fall of 1987. It put Midland, Texas, on the map. It was the kind of week that none of us would ever like to live through again.

It was early on a Wednesday morning in October. I had just arrived at the office. I was reading a press release about some local fund-raising event when the telephone rang. It was Ed Wilson. Ed is the owner of the sporting goods store just down the street.

"Did you hear about Chip McClure's little girl?" he asked. "The poor child fell down a well shaft. Right in Chip's sister-in-law's back yard!"

Chip McClure had been working at Ed's store for nearly a year. He was only eighteen years old. He had married Cissy, his high school sweetheart, when the two of them were still sophomores at Midland High. Their daughter, a beautiful little girl named Jessica, was just eighteen months old that October. I could only imagine how Chip and Cissy were feeling at that moment. I shuddered, picturing little Jessica at the bottom of a well shaft.

I drove to the old gray house where Cissy McClure's older sister lived. By the time I arrived, more than a dozen police officers and firefighters were already on the scene. I asked a cop I knew to fill me in on what had happened.

The cop gave me a step-by-step rundown. He'd seen a lot in his time. But as he told this story, I could see that his hands were shaking. He told me that Cissy and her sister were taking care of a few of the neighborhood kids while their folks were working. Around nine o'clock that morning, Cissy stepped inside the house to answer the telephone. While she was inside, Jessica decided to explore around the back of the house.

What little Jessica found out back was an eight-inch-wide opening in the ground. Apparently, she thought it would be fun to dangle her feet over the edge. The opening led to an old well shaft that had been abandoned long ago. As luck would have it, the rock that covered the shaft was knocked loose when little Jessica stood up. The poor little thing found herself tumbling twenty-two feet down a dry well shaft.

News spreads fast in a town like Midland. Within minutes, folks were practically tripping over one another trying to help the McClures rescue their toddler. Unfortunately, Jessica was too far down the narrow shaft simply to be pulled out.

For the rest of that day, the sleepy town of Midland was in a state of emergency. Teachers stopped teaching, kids stopped playing, and parents stopped making dinner. Everybody's mind was on Jessica, hoping beyond hope that her life could be saved.

Rescue workers decided to drill another shaft right next to the old well. They could then dig a tunnel across to reach the trapped child. West Texas is oil country, and finding a drilling rig wasn't much of a problem. Still, it was going to take some time to dig through that hard, rocky ground.

First and foremost was the need to get fresh air and a kind voice to the child. They lowered oxygen hoses into the hole so Jessica could breathe. Then a microphone was dropped down so that Cissy and Chip could talk to their terrified baby. Cissy stood by the mike all that day. She was fighting back tears as she sang one song after another to her poor little girl. As I watched, I couldn't keep my own tears from welling up. The feeling of being unable to save her tore me up inside.

Well, I'm here to tell you that the people of Midland never stopped to rest for a second. They worked all day long, trying to dig their way down to that little girl. At dusk, floodlights were set up. The digging continued through the entire night.

Our town's aching heart and tireless energy put it on the map. By morning, over a hundred reporters and photographers from all over the country had gathered around the site. Americans from coast to coast were watching and hoping that the little baby would be saved. It seemed as if the whole world cared about the little girl they called Baby Jessica.

Digging down was tough and discouraging. But when they started on the connecting shaft, things got worse. They had to fight their way through solid rock. It was a grueling job. All of it had to be done by hand. Luckily, there were plenty of volunteers who were eager to help.

Friends and neighbors took turns climbing up and down the shaft to do the digging. Little by little, they were getting closer to that little girl. Time was running out, though. Jessica had been down there for almost two whole days.

Finally, on Friday afternoon, two long days after the ordeal began, there was a breakthrough. A paramedic named Robert O'Donnell crawled through the tunnel in the hope of bringing Jessica out. The crowd at the well was frozen with anticipation. "Please, let him reach her!" someone blurted out to no one in particular.

You should have heard the groans of disappointment when he climbed out alone! He had been able to reach in and touch the girl. But the tunnel wasn't quite wide enough to bring her out safely. So, the slow process of digging through solid rock went on.

Almost fifty-nine hours had passed, and Baby Jessica still lay at the bottom of that terrible well. Bursts of sobbing came from people in the crowd who didn't even know Jessica or her family.

Suddenly, a paramedic named Steve Forbes emerged from the tunnel. In his arms, swaddled in white gauze bandages and covered with mud, was Baby Jessica.

A cheer of delight went up from that weary crowd. "He's got her!" I heard voices shout in jubilation. Others sounded more cautious. "Is she OK?" they whispered. "Is she going to live?"

The joy, excitement, hope, and worry of the crowd were like nothing I'd ever seen before. As an ambulance rushed Jessica and her weeping parents to Midland Memorial Hospital, church bells rang all over town. I rushed back to my office to begin typing the story as I'd seen it firsthand. Then I realized that I couldn't finish that story without knowing how the child was doing.

You can imagine my relief when I found out that Baby Jessica was in good condition. She'd lost some weight, and her head was scraped up pretty badly. All things considered, though, this ending was a whole lot happier than anyone had a right to expect.

By the time my story came out, every major newspaper in the world had also printed it on their front pages. All the big-city dailies had sent reporters and photographers to our little town to interview Cissy and Chip. Baby Jessica's face looked out from every television screen in the world.

Workmen sealed up that open well with a permanent metal cap. Eventually, a plaque was put up to remind the world about the ordeal that the McClure family had endured for three dreadful days in October.

What about our little hometown paper? Had I really written the whole story? As the days passed, I began to doubt it. The saving of Baby Jessica was exciting enough. Still, what was waiting to be told wasn't just about Jessica and Cissy and Chip. The story I needed to tell was the story of a community. It was the story of people banding together to meet a crisis head-on. I'm talking about people who are willing to take a shovel in hand and crawl down a dark hole at night to save a little girl they don't even know.

To some folks, being warmhearted means mailing out a check once or twice a year to some organization that promises to help buy clothes and food for the needy. That's all well and good, but there's a face-to-face type of kindness that most people never get a chance to experience.

Maybe there's nothing special about our little town. I don't care if there's not. Ever since that week, I've been awfully proud to say I come from Midland. During those terrible three days in October, we showed the world what it truly takes to be a good neighbor. We showed them what it means to be a hero.

READING FOR UNDERSTANDING

1. Arrange the following incidents in the order in which they occurred:
   (a) The reporter wrote a story about Baby Jessica.
   (b) Baby Jessica was rushed to the hospital.
   (c) The rock covering the shaft was knocked loose when Jessica stood up.
   (d) A young paramedic crawled into the shaft in an effort to save Baby Jessica.
   (e) Baby Jessica fell down the well.
2. Why was Jessica so hard to reach after she fell down the well?
3. How did Jessica's mother try to comfort her when she was in the well?
4. What condition was Jessica in when they finally rescued her?
5. Why do you think a plaque was put up over the well?
6. How does the reporter's focus change at the end of Baby Jessica's ordeal?

RESPONDING TO THE STORY

Neighbors responded in various ways to the emergency in Midland, Texas. How would you have responded? In what ways might you have tried to help? Write your response in paragraph form.

REVIEWING VOCABULARY

Match each word on the left with the correct definition on the right.

1. grueling	**a.** wrapped in cloth
2. ordeal	**b.** painful experience
3. paramedic	**c.** emergency medical worker
4. blurted	**d.** exhausting and difficult
5. swaddled	**e.** piece of metal with lettering
6. plaque	**f.** deep opening
7. shaft	**g.** said suddenly
8. welling	**h.** place
9. site	**i.** pouring forth; gushing

THINKING CRITICALLY

1. If an adult had been trapped in the well, newspaper and television coverage as well as the reaction of the people of the United States might have been different. Describe how you think that people and the media might have reacted to an adult trapped in a well. Why would the reaction be different?

2. Why do you think that so many people were interested in the story of Baby Jessica? Does this change your opinion of people? Explain.

3. Do you think that the Baby Jessica experience changed the town of Midland, Texas? If so, how?

A LIFE FOR
A LIFE

Dina Anastasio

Mining for coal is dangerous, dirty work. Miners run the risk of breathing dangerous gases and fumes. Even worse, the tunnels in mines are fragile and can easily collapse, trapping the workers hundreds of feet below the surface of the earth.

The life of a miner is tough. But sometimes friendship can ease the burden. The story you are about to read is about two miners who are best friends. Both must struggle against the odds after their mine collapses. One miner faces a choice—whether to save his own life or risk his life to help his friend. He has to make his decision as quickly as possible. Otherwise, both men may die.

VOCABULARY WORDS

cascading (kas-KAYD-ing) pouring or falling in a series
❖ Have you ever seen the *cascading* waters of Niagara Falls?

instinctively (ihn-STIHNK-tihv-lee) naturally, without thinking.
❖ *Instinctively*, I jumped away from the hot flames.

debris (deh-BREE) broken bits and pieces
❖ After the rock slide, a bulldozer was needed to clear all the *debris* from the highway.

gloom (GLOOM) dimness or darkness
❖ Straining their eyes, they tried to see through the *gloom*.

urgency (UHR-juhn-see) immediate need for action
❖ He spoke with *urgency* about the need to repair the community center.

frantically (FRAN-tihk-lee) excitedly and fearfully
❖ *Frantically*, she bolted the door to keep out the suspicious-looking person.

composure (kuhm-POH-zhuhr) calmness
❖ Although the troops were under enemy fire all day, Major Innis never lost his *composure*.

**Jimmy Peters** was walking slowly through the main tunnel toward the entrance of the coal mine. His long shift was over and he was dirty and exhausted. He observed his best friend Alek enter the mine and walk in his direction. Alek's shift was about to begin. Suddenly, without warning, one of the large support beams above them snapped and the mine collapsed.

Jimmy understood exactly what had happened. There was no need to cry out or shout for help. As soon as the rocks began to fall in front of him, he knew that he was in serious trouble. The rocks were cascading down between him and the entrance to the mine.

"Look out, Jimmy!" Alek shouted. "Get out of the way!" Instinctively, Alek moved towards Jimmy, but the rocks and debris were falling too quickly between them. If he got too close to Jimmy, he certainly would be crushed. Yet he had to do something immediately, because a wall was beginning to form between them.

Alek turned and glanced quickly behind him. The rays from the late-afternoon sun were shining faintly through the entrance. The other miners were anxiously calling to him from the entrance.

"Come out! Come out!" they were shouting. "Hurry, Alek! Get out of there now!" But Alek was not about to budge. His best friend was on the other side of that wall, and he wasn't going to abandon him.

The rocks suddenly had stopped falling, and the mine was quiet. A wall was now created between Alek and Jimmy that was much too high to climb.

"Jimmy?" Alek yelled, his voice coming back at him in strange echoes. "Are you there? Are you all right?"

Alek stood there alone, waiting nervously for his friend to answer. He heard only silence. A voice inside

21

his head seemed to shout: "Get out before the rocks fall
again!" But Alek just moved closer to the wall.

He called out urgently: "Are you there, Jimmy? Can
you hear me?" Again there was no answer. For one long
moment, Alek wondered if his best friend was dead.

Jimmy Peters was not dead. His left leg was trapped
beneath a large wooden beam, and total blackness surrounded him. The wall in front of him was so thick
that he could hear nothing at all.

Jimmy Peters was far from dead but he felt completely and utterly alone. Above him, the mine was
beginning to crumble once again. He expected to be
crushed at any moment, and there was nothing that he
could do about it.

Jimmy shifted his shoulders on the cold earth and
wondered about Alek. He sincerely hoped that his
friend had managed to get out safely.

"I've got to get out of here!" Jimmy thought, beginning to feel desperate. "I've got to get out of here fast.
How on earth can I do it?" He sat up and put all his
energy into moving the beam. It was no use. His leg
was pinned to the ground. If he was going to live,
someone would have to save him. There was no possible way that he could save himself.

On the other side of the wall, Alek was still calling
out to Jimmy. Jimmy was silent. Alek concluded that
either Jimmy was dead or the wall was very thick. He
wondered how thick the wall really was and whether
he still had enough time to dig his friend out of there.

The mine was crumbling fast now. It wouldn't be
long before it would collapse completely. Alek glanced
once more over his shoulder at the entrance, where the
sun's rays barely pierced the gloom. His fellow miners
still were waiting there, shouting his name with
increasing urgency, over and over again.

"Get out, Alek!" they were hollering. "You know you can't save him, so just get out now!"

Alek took a deep breath and slowly let the air out. He looked behind him at the faint rays of the sun, then turned and studied the giant wall that separated him from his friend. After that, he went to work.

One by one, the rocks came loose in his hands. Frantically, he grabbed at the wall, pulling it apart. It seemed as if there was no end to the wall, as if it just continued on and on forever.

"I'm coming, Jimmy!" he shouted, as he quickly dug his way through the thick mass of rock and debris. "I'm coming for you!" he kept calling out.

Something was falling behind his back. He quickly looked over his shoulder, as a cascade of rocks dropped directly behind him. In a very short time, another wall could block him from the entrance to the mine. But Jimmy was still waiting to be rescued, so Alek turned back and continued clawing madly at the wall.

Suddenly, in the middle of digging, he hesitated. He thought he heard a muffled sound. He placed his ear against the mountain of debris and listened. There was no mistaking that noise! It surely was the sound of someone groaning. "Jimmy!" he shouted.

"Hurry, Alek!" Jimmy called back, his voice betraying both relief and fear. "The mine is going again."

"Help me dig!" Alek pleaded with him. "Dig from your side!" Another small pile of rocks cascaded down behind him. Alek dug faster, until he had made himself a hole deep enough to squeeze through. He wiggled through to the other side, bent down over his friend, and immediately understood why his friend hadn't been able to help him dig through the wall.

"No wonder you couldn't dig," he said to himself quietly, when he saw the large wooden beam on

Jimmy's leg, keeping him a prisoner. Jimmy glanced up at his friend and smiled a trembling smile. It took him a moment to regain his composure. "How many others are trapped?" he asked weakly, fearing the response.

Alek, relieved at seeing his friend alive, laughed nervously. "You're the only one. But the mine's shaky, so we have to get you out of here fast."

"I'm afraid I can't be of much help," Jimmy replied, sighing and looking at the beam on top of his leg.

Lifting and pushing with all his might, Alek somehow was able to move the beam off Jimmy's leg. Leaning over, he gently helped his trembling friend to his feet and asked, "Is the leg broken?"

Jimmy stepped down hesitantly and tried to walk. He took one step, then another, and another, until he was sure that the leg was only bruised and not broken.

Alek showed him how to climb through the hole, and cautioned, "Careful, it's not a very solid wall, Jimmy. If you knock it down, it may be the end of us both. I'll go first."

Alek climbed through carefully. It would take Jimmy longer to go through with his injured leg. On the other side, Alek could see the sun shimmering brightly outside the entrance to the cave. He stopped for a moment to enjoy it. Then he glanced back at Jimmy. Jimmy was still struggling through the hole in the wall.

The other miners were shouting Alek's name and cheering him on from the outside.

"Alek! Alek!" they cried. "Get a move on, Alek!"

More rocks were falling between the entrance and Alek. The people at the entrance knew that the mine would soon collapse completely. "Hurry, Alek!" they shouted. "Get out of there!"

Jimmy was still only halfway through the hole. Alek wondered if Jimmy's foot was stuck. Alek hurried back to the wall to help Jimmy all the way through. Then, as they were moving toward the entrance, the roof collapsed.

Alek and Jimmy covered their heads as the rubble poured down in front of them. Before they knew it, they were facing another wall. This time, however, they were together. Within seconds, they were attacking the new wall of rubble.

They weren't alone, because the miners were also digging at the rocks on the other side of the wall. "We'll get you out of there!" the miners were shouting. "Just another minute! Hang on! Keep digging, boys, and you'll be out of there in one minute flat!"

There were so many miners digging that they had Jimmy and Alek out of the mine in less than a minute. Inspired by Alek's rescue of Jimmy, they had worked furiously to free them.

Finally, Jimmy and Alek were outside. The sun was sparkling, and the sky was a brilliant blue. Jimmy and Alek collapsed together onto the grass.

They didn't say anything for a long time. Finally, Jimmy said in a shaky voice, "Thanks, I'll never forget what you did for me."

Alek shot a confused glance at his friend. "What did I do?" he asked.

"You saved my life," Jimmy responded.

Alek shrugged and grinned. "Well, what was I supposed to do, leave you there? Anyway, you saved my life, too."

"I guess that's what friends are for," Jimmy declared.

Alek nodded. "I guess so," he answered.

READING FOR UNDERSTANDING

1. Arrange the following incidents in the order in which they occurred:
   (a) Alek and Jimmy covered their heads as the rubble poured down between them and the mine entrance.
   (b) Alek pleaded with Jimmy to help him dig from the other side.
   (c) After his shift was over, Jimmy walked through the mine's main tunnel toward the entrance.
   (d) Jimmy thanked Alek for saving his life.
   (e) Jimmy's left leg became trapped.
2. Why did Alek refuse to abandon Jimmy?
3. As Jimmy lay trapped, what thoughts ran through his mind that showed how he felt about Alek?
4. While the two men were moving toward the entrance of the mine, what new crisis did they have to face?
5. In your own words, explain the meaning of the title of the story.

RESPONDING TO THE STORY

Both friends in the story found that they had to depend on each other to survive. Have you ever felt that you needed to depend completely on another person? In a paragraph, describe the situation and your feelings about it.

REVIEWING VOCABULARY

Match each word on the left with the correct definition
on the right.

1. urgency   **a.** dimness or darkness
2. debris   **b.** naturally, without thinking
3. composure   **c.** pouring
4. cascading   **d.** excitedly and fearfully
5. gloom   **e.** broken bits and pieces
6. instinctively   **f.** immediate need for action
7. frantically   **g.** calmness

THINKING CRITICALLY

1. This story suggests that the most important quality
   in a friend is *loyalty*. Do you agree? What other
   qualities should one look for in a friend?
2. Is loyalty to a friend always a good idea? Think of
   several situations in which you might say no to a
   friend's request.
3. How do you think that Alek and Jimmy feel about
   the response of the other miners to the urgent situation? How do you think Jimmy felt about their
   trying to get Alek to run out of the mine after it
   first collapsed?

A QUEST THROUGH THE JUNGLE

Carroll Moulton

What kinds of skills do you use to stay healthy, alive, and out of trouble in the town or city where you live? Now imagine suddenly finding yourself in the jungle. Would the same skills keep you safe and well? In the following story, this is exactly what a young man will find out.

The young man is an engineer working in Panama. Suddenly, he finds himself in a jungle full of danger. When the unexpected occurs, he must act quickly. Frightened as he is, he pushes on in search of the one thing that can help him. Will he make it? Read to find out.

VOCABULARY WORDS

engineer (ehn-juh-NIHR) person who designs machinery, road systems, bridges, or canals
❖ The finest *engineer* in the country helped plan the building of that bridge.

apparatus (ap-uh-RAT-us) tools, instruments, or device
❖ The milking machine was part of the farmer's *apparatus*.

forded (FAWRD-ehd) walked across the shallow part of a river
❖ The water was only ankle deep at the spot where they *forded* it.

quinine (KWY-nyn) substance used to treat malaria
❖ Doses of *quinine* brought the fever down.

carcass (KAHR-kuhs) dead body of an animal
❖ The *carcass* of the mouse was decayed.

rodent (ROHD-uhnt) animal that gnaws with sharp front teeth
❖ A rat is considered to be a *rodent*.

KEY WORDS

Panama (PAN-uh-maw) country in Central America
Teddy Roosevelt (TEH-dee ROH-zuh-vehlt) president of the United States from 1901–1909
❖ President *Teddy Roosevelt* supported a revolution in *Panama* that led to the building of the Panama Canal.

mestizo (mehs-TEE-zoh) person with one parent from Spain and one Native American parent.
❖ He was a *mestizo* because his mother was Spanish and his father was a Native American.

 **M**any years ago in 1904, only a short time after I'd finished college, fate put me down in the middle of a jungle in Panama. It should have been a young engineer's dream job: assistant to the chief engineer of the Canal Commission.

Panama was a brand-new country then. It had declared independence from Colombia only six months before we landed there. President Teddy Roosevelt had approved the construction of the canal. People said that if we could pull it off, it would be an engineering miracle. So the offer to go down to the tropics seemed like a dream come true. I didn't know then that one part of the job would turn out to be a nightmare.

One of our first jobs was to branch out from the canal route into the jungle, surveying possible supply routes. On these expeditions, which usually lasted a week or so, we traveled with a partner and a guide.

The trip that I'll never forget started out smoothly enough. My partner was a surveyor named Marcus Topalian, about three years older than I, from St. Louis. Marcus was a big, lean fellow with red hair who had played football in college. He was six foot five. He had arrived in Panama a couple of months before me. Before he got into survey work, he studied medicine. The Canal Commission had sent him out a few times with Colonel Gorgas, the U.S. Army doctor who was trying to wipe out malaria and yellow fever in Panama.

Marcus met me in Cristobal. We picked up Hipolito, our guide, in Margarita. Hipolito was a *mestizo*, but he looked mostly Indian. He was fluent in English, Spanish, and French. He also claimed to know the territory between Margarita and Escobal. This was the first trip I'd made with him. I liked him right away.

The plan was to move south to where they were to build the big dam on the Chagres River. We knew that it would be slow going, so we traveled as lightly as we could. Still, with our bedrolls, cooking supplies, canteens, and surveying apparatus, we each carried a pack of over forty pounds.

By the third day, we'd made good time and reached the Chagres. As we forded a shallow part of the river, I slipped and went under. The water was only chest deep, but the current was strong. I had to struggle to get back upright under the weight of my pack.

It was not till we stopped for the day that I noticed that one flap on the backpack was loose. The first-aid kit was missing. We weren't concerned, however. After all, we'd be back in Colon in four days.

Then, later that evening, Marcus's behavior began to worry me. He'd been feeling run-down for the past few days. After supper he suddenly started to shiver. Several blankets failed to warm him. His body shook wildly. Hipolito frowned.

"Has this happened before, Marcus?" he asked.

"Once or twice, when I was out with Colonel Gorgas last month. It wasn't this bad."

The guide turned to me. "George, there's no way to be sure, but I'm worried. These shakes could be the first sign of malaria."

One night later, we all knew that Hipolito was right. For eight hours, Marcus had suffered a malarial attack.

First, was shaking and chills. Then the shakes had given way to a high fever. Just before sunrise, the fever turned to sweats that drenched the bedroll. Around nine o'clock, his temperature came down. Finally, Marcus could sleep a little.

Hipolito and I cooked breakfast. We tried to decide what to do. I felt guilty and responsible. The one thing that could help Marcus had been in that pack. It was the quinine. And I had lost it.

Hipolito tried to reassure me. He was certain that Marcus would make it, even though he was too weak to travel. We needed to get help as soon as possible. The next attack could be worse. It might even kill him, and it was likely to occur within a day or two.

Hipolito decided to leave me with Marcus and get back to Margarita as fast as he could. There he would organize a rescue party. This meant I'd be alone with Marcus for about three days.

Before he left, Hipolito told me that there was quinine in the rain forest, if I could find it. The bark and roots of the cinchona tree were the source of quinine. While the quinine wouldn't cure Marcus, it would help control the fever attacks.

Hipolito described what the cinchona tree looked like. He said that it was a tall tree, like an evergreen. The trunk could be thicker than a man's body. The easiest way to recognize the tree was by the flowers. They were small and white and mixed with rosy purple. They looked like lilac blossoms.

After Hipolito left, I waited for Marcus to wake up. Then I explained everything. He was so weak that I hated to leave him. He urged me to go while there was still light. He assured me that he'd be fine. I cooked some food and gave him lots of blankets. Then I set out on my quest through the jungle.

I'd grown up on the streets of South Boston, so I didn't have much wilderness experience to rely on. Hipolito had told me to head due east. I was to stop when the land sloped upward and the forest gave way to a grassy area.

I had a compass, of course. During the day, the sun would help guide me. But how would I find my way back, especially after dark? I soon realized that my greatest problem was to avoid getting lost. There was only one thing to do: mark the trail by bending twigs or making scratches on trees.

To help Marcus, I had less than twenty-four hours to find the cinchona. By five o'clock, I knew that I would spend my first night alone in the jungle. Although I had a rifle to defend myself, it was the unknown that made me nervous. A rifle was no help against the mosquitoes that spread malaria and yellow fever.

I had one more hour of good light. The jungle grew strangely quiet. When I entered a clearing, I shuddered. The huge, half-eaten carcass of an animal lay there. From the size of the body and the shape of the head, it looked like a hundred-pound gerbil. As I stared, some turkey vultures looked up at me, bits of meat hanging from their beaks.

Perhaps it was just as well that I didn't know all the details at the time. Hipolito later told me that what I'd seen was a capybara, the world's largest rodent. Most likely it had been killed by a jaguar, who had then left the carcass.

The awful sight of the birds feeding turned out to be a stroke of luck. I watched as more vultures flew down to feed. Then—there they were! About twenty-five feet up were those tiny white and purple blossoms. Cinchona!

Hipolito hadn't told me how much bark to strip from the tree. So I cut as much as I could carry. The hard part was waiting out the night before retracing my route back to Marcus. With visions of the carcass and the vultures, I slept very little.

I kept walking all of the next day. The bark seemed to grow heavier and heavier. At one point I couldn't find the markings I'd left and began to panic. I lost the trail. Then, just before dark, I caught sight of a bent twig I'd planted. I knew I was back on track again.

When I got back to Marcus the next morning, the fever had not yet returned. He told me how to grind the bark into a powder, which then could be mixed with water from our canteens. We had no idea how much he should take. We thought that he could take sips when an attack came on. Then he could keep sipping until the chills and fever decreased.

We used the cinchona on the second night, when Marcus had an attack. At first, the drug had no effect. Marcus's fever soared, and he grew delirious. He acted as though he were losing his mind. I wondered if he would make it. But I held the canteen to his lips and urged him to sip. An hour passed. His forehead felt even hotter.

By the middle of the night, the quinine had worked. The fever was under control! Marcus's delirium passed. He even was able to sit up and recognize me. I knew, though, that if help didn't come soon, we would run out of quinine. I stayed awake all night, hoping to hear human footsteps.

Then, a few hours after dawn, I heard a crashing through the underbrush. Was it the jaguar that had killed the capybara? Would we be his next target? Imagine my relief when I saw the smiling face of Hipolito. He had returned with medicine, a stretcher, and a rescue party of four. Within two and a half days, we moved Marcus out of the jungle and into a hospital in Margarita. His life was saved!

READING FOR UNDERSTANDING

1. What reason did the narrator of the story give for being sent to Panama?
2. What did the narrator's partner, Marcus Topalian, look like?
3. Why did the narrator blame himself at first for not being able to help Marcus?
4. Why did Hipolito decide to leave the narrator and Marcus alone in the jungle?
5. Why did the narrator say that his job was "like a dream come true" that partly turned out to be a nightmare?
6. Why was the narrator glad that he hadn't known about the capybara when he saw it?
7. What does this story tell you about the skills that one needs to survive?
8. What do you think might have happened if the sounds of crashing through the underbrush had turned out to be the jaguar instead of the rescue party?

RESPONDING TO THE STORY

What scene in this story frightened you the most? Why? Have you ever had a frightening experience? Were you able to act wisely or did you "lose it"?

REVIEWING VOCABULARY

1. The *apparatus* of a barber includes **(a)** a car and a house **(b)** scissors and combs **(c)** shoes and socks.
2. If you saw the *carcass* of a bear, then the bear would be **(a)** dead **(b)** sick **(c)** eating.

3. If you had malaria and took *quinine*, it would
   (a) bring your fever down (b) make you sicker
   (c) cure you.
4. When people *ford* a river, they cross it at a (a) deep
   place (b) clean place (c) shallow place.
5. An *engineer* would help design (a) clothes
   (b) buildings (c) books.
6. An example of a *rodent* is a (a) jaguar (b) capybara
   (c) vulture.

THINKING CRITICALLY

1. What do you think of the way that the two men in
   this story worked together to save a life? Why is
   cooperation among people so important during difficult situations?
2. All three of the men in the story had character
   traits that helped them through the crisis. What
   were these traits, and how did they help?
3. How would you describe the narrator's character?
   He was the one who lost the quinine, but he was
   also the one who found another source of it. What
   do you like about him? Is there anything you don't
   like about him?

RIDING OUT THE STORM

Sandra Widener

On August 24, 1992, Hurricane Andrew slammed into southern Florida. Weather forecasters predicted the storm accurately. They gave the public plenty of warning, so the official death toll was very low for a powerful hurricane. Thousands of people lost their homes. The storm caused millions of dollars' worth of property damage.

With almost every hurricane, there are news stories about people who refuse to leave their homes. In the story that follows, young Sandro is caught in a bind. Hurricane Andrew is about to hit. Sandro has to get Aunt Juanita to leave her house before it's too late. But she refuses to leave. Read the story to see how Sandro handles the situation.

VOCABULARY WORDS

earnest (ER-nihst) sincere
❖ The man looked too *earnest* to be a liar.

exasperation (ihg-zas-puh-RAY-shuhn) great annoyance
❖ Her refusal to act was a source of *exasperation* to us.

jittery (JIHT-uhr-ee) nervous, fidgety
❖ Too much coffee can make you *jittery*.

shards (SHARDZ) fragments, or broken pieces
❖ When the vase fell, *shards* of glass flew everywhere.

predicament (prih-DIHK-uh-muhnt) difficult situation
❖ She helped us out of our *predicament*, and we were able to return home safely.

benignly (bih-NYN-lee) kindly
❖ The teacher smiled *benignly* as she gave out awards to the class.

laboriously (luh-BAWR-ee-uhs-lee) with great effort
❖ The engineers worked *laboriously* on the new tunnel design.

teeter (TEET-uhr) wobble
❖ The ladder started to *teeter*.

banked (BANKD) sloping of an airplane to avoid slipping sideways on a turn
❖ The helicopter *banked* before coming in to pick up the passengers.

**"Yes, Mom, *yes*, Mom,"** Sandro
replied, rolling his eyes as he held the tele-
phone receiver away from his ear and
looked at it. Then he put it back to his ear.
"No, Mom, I won't. Love you too, bye."

"Sheesh," Sandro said to Carmen as he hung up the
telephone. "You'd think this was the front lines in a war
or something, the way she talks. I mean, I am capable
of handling a week in Florida without my mother being
here. What does she think?"

"What's her problem?" asked Carmen.

"She's worried about the hurricane. She's dictating a
list a yard long of what to do if it hits. They're not even
sure Andrew's going to make it here."

"Sounds like it's a possibility," Carmen said. "Look."
She pointed to the television set. An earnest-looking
man was standing next to a map of Florida. On the
map, the coast was covered with white, swirling clouds.
Carmen turned up the volume.

". . . remember to take all precautions. This could be
a big one, folks."

"Shut it off," Sandro said, irritated. "I've got to work
on a report for my history class. Are you going to stay
awhile or are you going home?"

"I'm going. I've got to help my father in the yard,"
Carmen said. "But I'll see you soon."

The next morning, Sandro was awakened by the
telephone ringing. He sighed, picked it up, and said
"Hi, Mom," without waiting to hear who was on the
line. "Yeah, okay, I'll be sure to call her. Of course, I'll
be careful. Good-bye." Rubbing his eyes, he sat up,
yawned, and ran his fingers through his hair.

His mother wanted him to check on his great-aunt
Juanita. She lived out at the shore where Andrew was

likely to hit. Sandro's mother was afraid that Aunt Juanita wouldn't know what to do.

Ever since Aunt Juanita's husband had died, she wouldn't go anywhere. She spent all her time with an old dog she had found as a stray. Sandro's mother had begged Aunt Juanita to come north and live with them. Aunt Juanita refused and claimed she was through with human company. The death of her husband had left her seriously depressed.

After breakfast, Sandro switched on the television set. This time the TV reporter had a very serious expression on his face. He said that some of the people on the coast had been advised to move inland until the storm was over. Sandro ran to the telephone and dialed Aunt Juanita's number.

"Hello," he said. "It's Sandro. Are you doing okay out there, Aunt Juanita? Have they told you to leave the shore? What do you mean you're not going? Listen, I'm coming over right away!"

Sandro hung up and shook his head. "Has she gone mad?" he thought to himself. Everyone near that part of the shore had been told to move inland. But Aunt Juanita didn't plan to budge.

Aunt Juanita lived about a half hour's drive away. As Sandro drove over, he nervously twisted the radio dial, looking for some decent music. All the radio stations were issuing hurricane warnings. "Sounds like it's approaching," he thought to himself. "I'd better get her to a safe place!"

Aunt Juanita was sitting outside on the porch, her hands folded in her lap. This would have been fine except that it was raining furiously.

"Aunt Juanita, what are you doing out here?" Sandro called out, as he jumped out of the car and pulled his rain hood over his head.

"Hello, Sandro," she answered. "The weather sure is bad."

"No kidding," Sandro thought. "Aunt Juanita, we need to leave. The hurricane is coming! Please get into the car, and we'll find somewhere safe to wait out the storm."

Aunt Juanita's eyes looked empty and lifeless. "No," she said.

"No?" he asked in disbelief. He was beginning to panic. This storm was serious. "Come on, Aunt Juanita. Please get into the car."

"I'm staying here," she said stubbornly.

Sandro tried to reason with her. He begged and pleaded. She just looked at him, listened, and shook her head no. "I'm staying here until Carlito comes back. I can't leave without him."

Her words sent a shiver of horror through Sandro. Aunt Juanita really had gotten worse. Carlito was his uncle and her husband—and he was dead!

The wind was starting to whip up the trees, howling in time with the rain. The rain was falling so fast and furiously that it stung like needles when it hit his bare skin.

"Can't we at least go inside?" pleaded Sandro.

She nodded thoughtfully. "Yes, we can do that."

Sandro took her arm and led her inside. It was too late to leave now, anyway. He went back outside and fastened all the shutters securely. The wind was blowing so powerfully that he had trouble keeping his balance. By the time Sandro got inside, the electricity had gone out. The house was creaking and groaning, and the wind made a moan that terrified Sandro. Aunt Juanita was sitting there in a chair, smiling faintly, but looking dazed. Sandro looked at her and shook his head in exasperation. What was the matter with her?

"Listen, Aunt Juanita, we have to stay away from the windows. It's too bad you don't have a cellar, or an inside room!" Aunt Juanita shook her head sadly in agreement.

Sandro was getting jittery. She didn't seem to care what happened. Ever since her husband Carlito had died, Aunt Juanita didn't seem to care about anything. This time, as far as Sandro was concerned, she was going too far.

Suddenly, like bursts of machine-gun fire, two large windows blew out. Shards of glass flew everywhere, mingling with the rain, which was falling in sheets. Objects in the house were blown around the room.

Panicked, Sandro tried to think of what to do. He couldn't see any solution to their dangerous predicament. He sat with his head bowed for a moment. Suddenly, he sat upright.

Where was Aunt Juanita? He looked anxiously around the room. Aunt Juanita was sitting on the floor, looking confused. There was a tiny trickle of blood rolling down her forehead.

Sandro ran to her. "Are you all right?" he asked. He looked closely at her forehead. It was just a tiny cut, probably caused by one of the flying objects.

Aunt Juanita smiled at him benignly. "I hear Carlito," she beamed. "He's back." She stood and pushed past Sandro. He watched her walk toward the door.

Before he could stop her, she had pulled the door open. A tremendous blast of wind and rain knocked him backward and blinded his vision. Aunt Juanita was forced behind the door but tried to look outside. The blast stopped for a moment, and Sandro saw something small, wet, and hairy limping toward him. There was no time to decide what it was.

He pulled away from it and struggled toward the door. He pushed against it with all his might, but the wind and rain pushed back. Suddenly, a blast of air from the opposite window did the job for him. It slammed the door shut.

Sandro slid to the floor, gasping. Before him stood a whimpering dog. It was drenched and terrified. One of its legs must have been broken, for it stayed bent and hung limply above the other three.

"My Carlito's back!" said Aunt Juanita. It took Sandro a moment to realize what she meant. All this time, she hadn't been waiting for her husband. She'd been waiting for the stray dog she'd named after him!

There was a deafening, crackling sound. Sandro watched in disbelief as one side of the ceiling ripped away and went sailing. All three—Sandro, Aunt Juanita, and Carlito—fell to the floor. Sandro lay on his side and held onto the edge of a door frame. From time to time, he peeked up to see Aunt Juanita lying on her side against the cupboard, her arms clasped around the wailing stray. Rain, wind, and objects whipped around them.

Finally, the winds lessened, but the rain kept up. Sandro stood. The house was completely flooded. The water was almost up to his ankles. Aunt Juanita was standing on the only unbroken chair with the dog clasped in her arms.

Sandro looked upward and had an idea. Only half the roof had blown away. The other half was still attached. If they could get to the top of the roof, they might avoid drowning when the water rose.

Sandro saw Aunt Juanita's old paint-stained ladder on its side in the corner. Then he noticed that one leg of the kitchen table had broken off. By stacking books and broken pieces of wood under the table, he was able to get it to stand again. He piled more books and wood evenly onto the table surface to raise it at least another half-foot.

Sandro lifted the stepladder onto the platform he had made. He saw that it was just high enough to allow someone to reach the edge of the roof. But it felt shaky.

"Go ahead, Aunt Juanita," he said. "Climb up here to the roof, or we'll get drowned."

"Not without my Carlito, I won't," she snapped.

Sandro sighed but tried to remain calm. "You go first and I promise I won't leave Carlito behind," he said to her.

His great aunt looked suspicious. Then, this time—for once—she did what he said. Sandro held the ladder steady as she climbed laboriously toward the roof and hoisted herself over its edge.

Now it was time for him to fulfill his promise to her. He grabbed Carlito, who had crouched on the chair, shivering and looking terrified. "Take it easy, boy," said Sandro under his breath. Could he really make it up the ladder with a dog in one arm without tipping over?

Slowly, he climbed onto the tabletop and made his way up the ladder with the trembling dog clasped to his chest. At one point, the ladder started to teeter, but he steadied it by shifting his weight. Finally, he was able to hand the dog to Aunt Juanita and hoist himself onto the roof.

By morning, the water had risen almost to the roof. Sandro looked around Aunt Juanita's neighborhood with a kind of resigned terror. Everything was flooded. Only rooftops and the tips of a few trees could be seen. If the water kept rising, they wouldn't last must longer.

Then, miraculously, he heard the distinctive sound of a helicopter. It flew nearby, as Sandro frantically waved his arms. As he watched, the helicopter banked and flew away. He collapsed back onto the roof and buried his head on his arms in despair.

Then he heard the sound again. The helicopter was back. It circled above them and flew in closer. Someone waved, and Sandro saw a rope ladder flop down.

The helicopter moved in even closer so that the ladder was within his reach. He strained to catch it without falling into the water and missed the ladder. The helicopter flew in a circle and came back in, closer. This time Sandro grabbed the ladder. "Aunt Juanita," he shouted, "we're going to make it!"

She looked at him with a slight look of disbelief on her face. "Well, of course we are, Sandro. What did you think would happen?" He stared at her, his mouth open. Then he closed his mouth, smiled, and handed her the ladder.

"Just climb, Aunt Juanita," he said.

This time she didn't have to make him promise to take the dog. Calmly and deliberately, she climbed up into the waiting helicopter. Sandro waved his arms at the helicopter, pointing at the dog. Eventually, a rope with a small cloth sling attached to it was lowered. Sandro tied the sling tightly around Carlito. The man in the helicopter hoisted him up.

Then, the ladder came swinging by Sandro again. He grabbed it and began his climb. His heart was beating wildly—with relief!

READING FOR UNDERSTANDING

1. The main conflict for Sandro was **(a)** how to save Aunt Juanita **(b)** how to get out before the storm hit **(c)** how to contact his mother.
2. After the death of her husband, Aunt Juanita was **(a)** depressed **(b)** free to travel **(c)** closer to Sandro.
3. When Aunt Juanita first mentioned Carlito, Sandro thought that she meant **(a)** her dog **(b)** her dead husband **(c)** the mayor.
4. From details in the story, we can assume that Sandro, Aunt Juanita, and Carlito were on the roof **(a)** half an hour **(b)** an hour **(c)** all night.
5. Aunt Juanita's words and actions seemed to Sandro that she was **(a)** very sensible **(b)** trying to be funny **(c)** not living in reality.
6. From hints in the story, about how old do you think Sandro was? **(a)** in his late teens **(b)** in his early teens **(c)** in his mid-twenties.

RESPONDING TO THE STORY

Choose one event, statement, or image in the story that made an impression on you. Why is it meaningful? Explain your response in a paragraph.

REVIEWING VOCABULARY

The following sentences are based on the story. Decide which of the words following the sentences best fits each blank. Write your answers on a separate sheet of paper.

1. The TV weather forecaster looked _____.
2. Sandro grew _____ at the thought of the approaching hurricane.

3. He shook his head in _____.

4. When the windows blew out, _____ of glass flew everywhere.

5. When Aunt Juanita heard Carlito, she smiled

_____.

6. Sandro steadied the ladder when it started to

_____.

7. Aunt Juanita climbed up the ladder _____.

8. Sandro thought about how to escape from their

_____.

Words: *benignly, earnest, exasperation, jittery, laboriously, predicament, shards, teeter*

THINKING CRITICALLY

1. How did Sandro behave when he believed that Aunt Juanita had lost her mind? Do you think he was right?

2. How was the dog important to the story? What did Aunt Juanita's feeling for the dog show about her character?

3. Did Sandro respect his aunt's wish to save Carlito? What did that show about him?

4. If you were Sandro, would you have behaved as he did during the hurricane? What might you have done differently? Why?

Unit 2
TRIAL BY FIRE

TWIN TOWER ESCAPE

Cecilia Rubino Lucas

The following story is based on a real-life crisis in New York City. On Friday, February 26, 1993, a bomb explosion in one of the twin towers of the World Trade Center forced the evacuation of the building.

Flames and smoke spread swiftly upward. Thousands of workers poured out of one of the tallest buildings in the world. The amazing part of this emergency was that the crowd behaved so calmly. There were many cases of quiet heroism. People stopped to help one another. Read on to see how Yolanda Lopez, five months pregnant, survived the skyscraper horror—with the help of a coworker.

VOCABULARY WORDS

converging (kuhn-VERJ-ihng) meeting
❖ The sight of the three rivers *converging* was impressive.

format (FAWR-mat) layout, arrangement
❖ The lawyer was careful to draw up the contract in the proper *format*.

agitated (AJ-uh-tayt-uhd) upset, excited
❖ The storm reports made us more and more *agitated*.

prenatal (pree-NAYT-uhl) happening before birth
❖ During her pregnancy, she was very attentive to her baby's proper *prenatal* care.

maneuvered (muh-NOO-vuhrd) moved skillfully
❖ The halfback *maneuvered* through a gap in the defensive line and ran for a touchdown.

pitched (PICHT) fell headlong
❖ Cindy lost her balance on the ice and *pitched* forward into a snowdrift.

asthma (AZ-muh) breathing disorder
❖ Their child suffered badly from *asthma*.

toxic (TAHK-sihk) poisonous
❖ After the chemical explosion, *toxic* fumes were a serious threat to the neighborhood.

acrid (AK-rihd) bitter, stinging
❖ The thick, *acrid* smoke injured some of the firefighters.

Could it be starting to snow again?
Yolanda Lopez looked out her window on
the 103rd floor. Sometimes it was difficult
to tell from this height what the weather
was like. When Yolanda had first inter-
viewed for the job as a legal assistant for Federated
Savings Bank, she wasn't sure if she was going to like
working almost at the top of the World Trade Center.
She hadn't counted on the breathtaking view. After five
years, she still loved to look at the Statue of Liberty
holding up her torch and at the Hudson and East rivers
converging. Yolanda glanced back at her computer
screen, but she was too hungry to keep working. It was
just past noon. She had to get some lunch. Yolanda was
five months pregnant. It didn't matter how much she
ate for breakfast. By midday she was always starving.

"Yolanda, here are those figures you asked for," Li
Ying, Yolanda's coworker, said as she dropped a sheet
of paper on her desk.

"Li, can you check this for me? Tell me if this format is OK."

"Sure." Li looked at Yolanda's computer screen.
"What's that rumbling?"

Yolanda responded, smiling, "That's my stomach
growling."

"I thought it might be the baby complaining," Li
replied, chuckling. "Come on, Yolanda. You're a pregnant woman. You can't work through lunch."

"You're right, but it's too cold to go out, and I didn't
have time to make a sandwich."

"I'll call the deli again," said Li Ying, picking up the
phone. Suddenly, the two women heard a thunderous
crash. The floor trembled under their feet. Then the
lights went out.

"That was definitely not your stomach." Li Ying put the phone down.

"Wow!" said Yolanda. "It sounded like a plane or a helicopter crashed into the building!"

Gloria, one of the secretaries, came rushing over to look out the window. The three women hurried to the other end of the office.

Mr. Fisher, their boss, stepped out of his office as the lights came back on. "Let's take a break until we find out what's going on. I'm sure it's nothing." Suddenly, smoke was coming in through the vents.

Gloria began coughing. "I don't know about the rest of you, but I'm getting out of here!" She turned on her heel and headed out the office door.

"I can't believe that nothing has been announced on the public address system. Why don't they tell us what's going on?" Li Ying was getting agitated.

Yolanda turned to Li Ying. "Let me call my husband. Maybe he knows something." She dialed, but no one answered.

"I can't reach him. Li Ying, what do you think we should do?" The office was filling with smoke. Smoke was even coming in through the light fixtures.

"I'm starting to think that Gloria is right. We shouldn't wait around to see what's going to happen. Let's just get out of here." Li Ying took Yolanda's arm. "Where's your coat?"

"It's over by my desk. We have to hurry!" Yolanda was coughing. "Breathing smoke like this can't be good for the baby."

"You have to prepare yourself, Yolanda. We're going to have to take the stairs. It's a long hike down. Do you think you can make it?"

Yolanda knew that if the power went out again, being stuck in one of the elevators would be the worst place to be. "I'll make it. I'm only in my fifth month, remember? I'm still going to my exercise class."

"A hundred flights is a little more stressful than a prenatal workout." Li Ying nervously slung her bag over her shoulder. "Let me carry your coat and bag. Bring your water bottle. And here, you should cover your mouth with this." Li Ying handed Yolanda a blue and white handkerchief. Then the two women headed for the office door.

Other workers were also making their way into the main hallway on the 103rd floor. Some were waiting at the bank of elevators. Li Ying steered Yolanda toward a side stairwell. She maneuvered through the crowd at the entrance, saying, "Pregnant woman! Please let us pass! Pregnant woman!"

No emergency lights were on in the narrow stairwell. The only light came from the open door to the hallway. People were backed up in the stairwell. Li Ying and Yolanda couldn't get through. It was like being crushed in a subway car at rush hour. Then the crowd started moving, though it was slow going at first. Everyone was orderly, walking single file down the stairs.

"When I was dreaming of leaving work early on Friday, this wasn't what I had in mind," Li Ying said.

Yolanda kept thinking that this shouldn't be happening. There are thousands of people on this staircase. We can't all get trapped here. Things like that happen only in the movies. The smoke was thick just above their heads. It was hard for Yolanda to breathe through the handkerchief that she had been holding over her mouth and nose.

Then the word came up the stairs that everyone should hold onto the shoulder of the person in front of him or her. As Yolanda reached out to grab on to Li

Ying's shoulder, Li Ying pitched forward in her high heels. Yolanda stumbled down a few stairs with her, as they bumped hard into the people in front of them. Yolanda screamed and covered her belly with her arms as she fell.

"Yolanda! Are you okay? Are you okay?" asked Li Ying, as she kicked off her shoes to prevent herself from falling again. With the help of a man in front of them, Li Ying got Yolanda to her feet.

"I'm okay. Let's not stop, Li Ying. I'm scared."

Then they all started down the stairs again. This time, Li Ying was next to Yolanda, supporting her arm, and Yolanda held on to the shoulder of the man ahead of her.

People were moving fairly quickly now. Only one man pushed ahead of them, saying, "Coming through, coming through." Everyone else was patient and orderly. They passed a woman who was having an asthma attack. Another woman was sharing her asthma medicine with her. With every step, Yolanda kept praying for her baby, praying that everything would be all right. The smoke smelled like burning tires. She wondered how toxic it was and if breathing in the smoke would hurt the baby.

Yolanda tried counting the steps, but she couldn't keep track of how many flights they'd climbed down. By about the fiftieth floor, everything was suddenly pitch-black. Even the bit of light that had been spilling in from the doorways was gone. No one had a flashlight. Yolanda was afraid of falling again. This is exactly what it's like to be blind, she thought. She couldn't see an inch in front of herself. Her knees began to tremble.

The smoke was getting thicker. "I don't know if we're going the right way," Yolanda said. "It seems like we're just heading down into the fire!" Yolanda rubbed her eyes. She began crying.

"You're going to make it. The baby is going to be okay, Yolanda. We just have to keep going," encouraged Li Ying.

"It can't be too much farther," the man in front of them said.

Suddenly, a light flashed up the stairs. A firefighter was climbing up the stairs, shining a flashlight. "Keep to the right, people. Clear the stairs on the left side. Rescue workers need to get through. Does anybody need help?"

Li Ying moved in front of Yolanda again. Suddenly, through the thick, acrid smoke, the women could see light at the bottom of the stairs. An hour and a half after starting down the stairs, they were finally outside! They stumbled into the cold, coughing. It was snowing! Yolanda took a sharp breath of fresh air and wiped the soot from her mouth and nose.

Li Ying wrapped a coat around Yolanda's shoulders, laughing and crying at the same time. "Yolanda, I'm sure everything's fine. Still, you should be examined by a doctor. Boy, we're really going to have a few stories to tell this kid when he gets here!"

"Hey, this could be a girl, you know!" Yolanda's knees wouldn't stop shaking.

"Then I'll tell her what an incredible mama she has!"

Yolanda noticed that Li Ying was standing in the snow without any shoes. "And I'll tell him or her what a great friend I have!"

READING FOR UNDERSTANDING

1. Arrange the following incidents in the order in which they occurred:

    (a) Yolanda fell down a few stairs.

    (b) Everything went pitch-black on the stairs.

    (c) Smoke started to come through the vents.

    (d) The women heard a thunderous crash.

    (e) A firefighter told everyone to keep to the right.

2. What details at the very beginning of the story show that Yolanda and Li Ying work well together at their job?

3. What were some of the precautions that Li Ying took before she and Yolanda started down the stairs?

4. How did the crowd behave during the emergency? What are some details that show that most of the people struggling to get out of the building helped one another?

5. What were some of Yolanda's thoughts as she went down the stairs? What did her thoughts reveal about Yolanda's personality?

RESPONDING TO THE STORY

Pretend that you are Yolanda and that it is six months after the events in the story. Write a letter to Li Ying. Tell her whether the baby is a boy or a girl. Also thank her for all the help that she gave you on the day of the emergency.

REVIEWING VOCABULARY

Match each word on the left with the correct definition on the right.

1. format	**a.** happening before birth
2. agitated	**b.** bitter, stinging
3. converging	**c.** moved skillfully
4. pitched	**d.** layout, arrangement
5. acrid	**e.** breathing disorder
6. maneuvered	**f.** upset, excited
7. toxic	**g.** fell headlong
8. prenatal	**h.** poisonous
9. asthma	**i.** meeting

THINKING CRITICALLY

1. Many action-adventure stories have male heroes. In this story, however, the heroes were women. In what ways did they seem different from male adventure heroes? In what ways did they seem the same?

2. What was there about Li Ying's character traits that made her a good friend? Find examples in the story to back up your answer.

3. The story is based on events that really happened in New York City. In the story, the people in the building behaved calmly and helped one another, just as people did on that scary Friday in 1993 at the World Trade Center. Do you think that you would have kept your head in such a situation? What would have helped you resist the temptation to panic?

RIVER OF DESTRUCTION

Dina Anastasio

Volcanoes can be difficult to predict. They can stay quiet for hundreds of years. Then suddenly, they may unleash their power. Burning, melting rock, ashes, and gases can shoot from their mouths, sometimes causing death and destruction.

Iceland, which lies in the North Atlantic Ocean near the Arctic Circle, has over 200 volcanoes on its main island and the islands around it. Some have been inactive for so many years that no one thinks about them anymore. However, this does not mean that they will not act up in all their fury someday. In the following story, set on a small island off Iceland, a sleeping volcano awakes.

VOCABULARY WORDS

erupted (ee-RUP-tihd) burst forth
* ❖ The volcano hasn't *erupted* for days.

engulfed (ehn-GULFT) swallowed up
* ❖ The family watched as flames *engulfed* their home.

cautioned (KAW-shuhnd) warned
* ❖ They *cautioned* us not to enter the cave.

surged (SERJD) moved forward like a wave
* ❖ When the doors opened, the angry crowd *surged* forward.

ooze (OOZ) flow or leak out slowly
* ❖ Blood started to *ooze* from the cut.

flotilla (floh-TIHL-uh) fleet of small ships
* ❖ The *flotilla* entered the harbor.

spewed (SPYOOD) threw up; gushed out
* ❖ The volcano *spewed* hot lava.

menace (MEHN-ihs) something that brings harm or danger
* ❖ Neighbors felt that his dog was a *menace*.

thwarted (THWAWR-tihd) defeated; kept from doing something
* ❖ The storms *thwarted* our plans.

 **J**ohnny Christianson was visiting his Uncle Peter on the island of Heimaey, off the coast of Iceland, when the volcano erupted. The year was 1973, and Johnny was 16 years old.

Johnny didn't know that there was a volcano on this little island. His uncle lived far away from it, near the harbor. No one had mentioned the volcano to Johnny. In fact, no one on the island had thought about the volcano for years.

Suddenly, the fiery hot rocks and ash were bursting from inside the cone. The eruption could be seen for miles, but at first, no one knew exactly what it was.

"It's a fire!" someone shouted.

Someone else replied: "No! It's an explosion. Looks like somebody's truck exploded."

As more and more people gathered to watch, the guesses became wilder and wilder. Within moments, it became clear that this was no simple fire or even a truck exploding. The ball of fire was shooting high up into the sky. People started to grow uneasy.

Then, as the flames continued and ash filled the air, the truth began to dawn on the inhabitants of the small island. The sleeping volcano had come to life!

Meanwhile, people who lived nearer the volcano already knew what was happening, and they were getting scared. As they watched in horror, the sky was filled with a tremendous black cloud of ash. A river of thick lava spilled from the edge of the crater. It poured down the side of the volcano, heading straight for town. And it was moving rapidly—at a speed of about a mile a minute.

Word of this spread to the farthest reaches of the island, and thousands of people headed for the sea.

Because they were fishing people, many had boats that could take them to Iceland. Uncle Peter was a fisherman, and so were most of Johnny's cousins. But their boat wasn't in the harbor. On this, of all days, his cousins were out fishing. They didn't even know about the eruption yet.

As the hot lava flowed toward town, it engulfed everything in its path. As soon as it touched bushes or trees, it knocked them down. The heat from the lava caused them to burst into flames.

As the lava came even closer to town, it began to destroy houses and stores. By this time, most of the people who lived in the village had fled. They piled into cars and trucks and headed for the sea.

The villagers huddled at the shoreline in fear and uncertainty. Some were already climbing into their boats. "There must be a way to stop it!" shouted someone. "It will destroy everything we own!"

But how could a river of hot lava be halted? How could they stop the spreading lava before it took over the whole island?

Everyone had an idea about how to stop the lava, but none of the ideas were very good. People were beginning to panic. Some of the boats were already heading for Iceland. And rescue boats were arriving from Iceland to pick up those who were stranded.

Some, however, weren't ready to leave. They had realized what would happen if the lava was allowed to flow into the harbor. It would stop the boats returning with the day's catch from landing. And if it filled up the harbor, it would ruin the fishing industry of the island for many years to come.

Johnny and his uncle were among the few people who were staying. His Uncle Peter remained calm. "Let's call in an expert," Uncle Peter suggested.

"We need a volcanologist who understands volcanoes and eruptions and lava flows."

Uncle Peter called the mayor of Heimaey, who quickly put in a call to Andrea Reyvik, a volcanologist at the university on the mainland.

"The answer may be cold water," Reyvik explained. "If you pour cold water on hot lava, the lava will immediately harden."

The mayor got off the phone and sprang into action. "Go and tell everyone left in the village to get hoses," he exclaimed to his assistants. "Get hoses and hose down the lava before it takes over the harbor. "But remember," he cautioned, "Andrea said that you have to start hosing down the lava way before it reaches the harbor's edge."

At this point, the lava was still at least a mile from the shore. The few people who had remained in the village brought buckets and hoses. They pumped cold water onto the sheet of molten lava.

Andrea Reyvik was right. Some of the lava hardened as soon as the cold water hit it. But the flow of lava was too wide and was traveling too fast to be stopped by their small hoses. A lot of it surged past the water and continued to ooze toward the sea.

The people gazed up at the sky and wished for the eruption to stop. If it would just stop, they might be able to block the lava flow before it poured into the harbor.

The lava was spreading through the town square now like frosting on a cake. Occasionally, a ribbon of flame burst from the flow. Then it would die out, only to be replaced by another. It was flowing evenly down the streets and heading straight for the sea.

"We need bigger hoses!" the townspeople cried. "Hurry, the lava has almost reached the harbor."

Standing on the dock in the harbor, Johnny and his uncle turned and looked toward the sea. The stream of lava had met the water now with a great hissing noise. Steam rose into the air. Johnny stood there for a long time, watching the molten rock flow into the harbor. He wanted to help, but there was nothing that he could do. There was nothing that anyone could do, because the water hoses were too small to stop this river of destruction.

Suddenly, Johnny noticed something interesting—something that just might save the day. A large boat was moving into the harbor, and several people on board were taking down huge hoses and pointing them at the lava. Soon, powerful jets of cold sea water poured down on the lava.

"Get in front of it!" Andrea Reyvik directed on the deck of the boat. "Point the hoses straight at its edge!"

"More hoses!" someone else hollered. "Line up and fire that water directly at it!"

A flotilla of small boats appeared in the harbor. Johnny's uncle peered anxiously through the spray of cold water and steam, searching for his sons' boat.

Suddenly, there it was, approaching the dock. The young men tied up their boat quickly and ran toward their father.

"Are you OK? How did you know about the volcano? Where's the catch?" Johnny and Uncle Peter shouted breathlessly as the young men approached them.

"We're fine," the boys responded. "We heard about the eruption when we stopped in Iceland. We left our catch there, but we rushed back here to help."

They all looked out to the harbor. The spray from the main boat's huge hoses was fantastic. It hit the lava right at its front edge and hardened it in seconds. As

63

soon as the lava cooled, Andrea and others left the boat and walked on it. They tiptoed gently at first, making sure that the lava was solid.

"Pipes!" Andrea announced, when she realized the hardened lava would hold them. "We need to put pipes inside the lava."

The townspeople brought pipes and sunk them deep inside the lava. When the pipes were in place, the people pumped cold water through the pipes, cooling the inside of the lava river. Now the lava was being cooled from the top and from the middle.

Everyone on the island—including Johnny, his Uncle Peter, and his cousins—worked for weeks to cool the lava and hold it back from the harbor.

"Do you think that volcano will ever stop erupting?" Johnny asked his uncle one night. He was exhausted from the work of the past few weeks, and there was still no end in sight.

"Of course it will," his uncle assured him. "Volcanoes don't erupt forever. Eventually they have to stop."

But the Heimaey volcano did not stop for another week. As it spewed more and more hot lava, the people who were trying to hold it off grew sick and weary. Larger ships with larger hoses were brought in to fight it. Day after day, cold water poured out of the hoses and bombarded the lava. But still it came.

Then, one day, the volcano stopped erupting, and the job became easier. The last of the lava finally stopped flowing. The water from the hoses attacked the last of the lava as it reached the harbor. At last, the whole river of lava had cooled and hardened. The battle against the fiery menace was over. The harbor had survived, but about a third of the town had been totally destroyed.

Slowly, as time passed, those who had fled Heimaey came back. They rebuilt houses and stores. They began to return to their normal activities. The volcano had grown quiet, and the fiery red menace had been thwarted. As the fishing boats chugged in and out of the harbor, the people noticed something new. A long arm of volcanic rock jutted out into the water. The boats moved around the point easily. The fishing industry on Heimaey had been saved.

Visitors to Heimaey may wonder how that long black point came to be there. But the people of Heimaey know. That point marks the very spot where the seemingly endless flow of lava was finally stopped in its tracks.

READING FOR UNDERSTANDING

1. Where, exactly, did this story take place?

2. Why was Johnny Christianson unaware of the volcano on the little island?

3. When the fire first erupted, what did everyone think?

4. When the people realized it was a volcano, why did they head for the sea?

5. Why did the villagers huddle at the shoreline in uncertainty? What decisions did they think of making?

6. Why do you think that Johnny and his uncle stayed on the island even after boats arrived to pick up the stranded villagers?

7. Describe in your own words the series of events that led to stopping the lava in its tracks.

RESPONDING TO THE STORY

Pretend that you are Johnny. Write a letter to your parents after the volcano has erupted. Describe what happened and how you felt. Give your opinion of your uncle's behavior during the crisis.

REVIEWING VOCABULARY

The following sentences are based on the story. Decide which of the words following the sentences best fits each blank. Write your answers on a separate sheet of paper.

1. In 1973, a volcano _____ on the island of Heimaey.

2. It _____ lava, which _____ everything in its path.

3. The mayor _____ them to get ahead of the lava.

4. The people pumped cold water on the lava, but it _____ past the water and continued to _____ toward the sea.

5. When a _____ came into the harbor, Uncle Peter his saw sons' boat.

6. The people of Heimaey finally _____ the fiery _____.

Words: *cautioned, engulfed, erupted, flotilla, menace, ooze, spewed, surged, thwarted*

THINKING CRITICALLY

1. Uncle Peter made several key decisions in this story. What were they? What did they show about his character?

2. The author used vivid language such as: "The lava was spreading through the town square now like frosting on a cake." Reread the story. Find other examples of vivid language. How did this vivid language affect your reading of this story?

3. Many places have famous monuments, such as a statue, to honor a local hero. In what way can the long black arm of volcanic rock be considered a monument to the people on the island of Heimaey?

COMING THROUGH THE FIRE

Eson C. Kim

Joon Lee is an ace mountain climber who is used to hiking alone. She is very talented and nearly fearless. Then along comes the day when those skills must be tested. Her very survival depends on it.

Joon is hiking in Yellowstone Park when a fire breaks out. She begins to panic, but realizes she must remain calm, if she wants to survive.

You may or may not have been in a situation as dangerous as the one Joon gets herself into. However, you have probably faced a situation when everything depended on your next move. How did you handle it? What did you do?

VOCABULARY WORDS

rappel (rah-PEHL) climb down, using a rope
❖ Before you go mountain climbing, you must be able to *rappel* down steep cliffs.

plateau (pla-TOH) high stretch of level land
❖ We hiked for miles across the *plateau*.

smoldering (SMOHL-der-ihng) burning and smoking without showing a flame
❖ The log in the fire had been *smoldering* for hours.

lumbered (LUHM-buhrd) moved clumsily
❖ The moose *lumbered* through the deep snow.

obstacle (AHB-stih-kuhl) something that is in the way
❖ The workers faced another *obstacle* in laying the railroad tracks.

subsided (suhb-SYD-uhd) became less; calmed down
❖ When the storm *subsided*, we went out to play baseball.

consumed (kuhn-SOOMD) used up or destroyed
❖ The horse *consumed* the whole bag of grain in less than an hour.

scorched (SKOHRCHT) damaged by burning
❖ One sleeve of his shirt was *scorched* by the candle flame.

KEY WORD

Yellowstone National Park (YEHL-oh-stohn NASH-uh-nuhl PAHRK) the oldest national park in the United States, located in Wyoming, Montana, and Idaho
❖ We went hiking in *Yellowstone National Park*.

 **O**ne **Saturday morning,** Joon Lee watched the August sun rise over Inspiration Point in Yellowstone National Park. Inspiration Point is a series of cliffs, with breathtaking views of the forested plains below.

Joon's bones were chilled from sitting on the bare, damp rock of the cliff, but she didn't mind. The sight of the warm, golden rays bathing the misty woods below more than made up for her minor discomfort.

Joon was looking forward to the peace of taking a hike alone. She was an experienced hiker and climber who had braved many situations. A couple of them had been close calls. She also had seen small forest fires. So she didn't even think twice about the growing clouds of smoke in the distance. As usual, the park officials and firefighters would keep everything under control.

After snapping a few photographs at Inspiration Point, Joon hiked south along the Yellowstone River. At one point, in order to get an unusual camera angle, she climbed a tree. It was then that she caught her second view of the distant fire. She could hardly believe it was the same fire that she had seen less than an hour ago.

Even from this distance, she could see the red-hot glow of the flames and the black puff of smoke. No fire that she had seen before had ever seemed this wild. She wondered if this was going to be serious. After all, this had been one of Yellowstone's driest summers.

Joon strapped on her backpack once more, planning to continue down the trail, but suddenly she was seized with the urge to get a better look at the fire. Returning to Inspiration Point would give her the best view. So she went back and climbed up to the highest cliff that she could find. The wind had picked up speed and carried with it some choking ash, which forced Joon to cough and rub her eyes. She looked out at the forested plains below. The line of flames in the distance was moving so fast that it looked like a flaming sword plunging through the forest.

Without warning, a thick cloud of blinding smoke rolled up to her. She could barely see the edge of the cliff. She was about to begin climbing down when she heard thumping noises behind her. Smoking chunks of charred wood were falling all around her. The wind was spreading these small seeds of fire everywhere.

The air cleared for a moment, and Joon looked fearfully at the flames. They had become a wall of fire that was moving closer by the second. Patches of fire were sprouting up in countless other areas as well.

If the fire had spread this quickly in a matter of minutes, Joon knew that she had even less time to get down from this perch before the flames reached her. The trail that led down the cliff was already on fire. She would have to rappel down the side of the plateau.

Joon tied one end of the rope around her waist. She looped the rope around the trunk of a tree. Then she wrapped an extra shirt around her right thigh for padding. She was excellent at rappelling. She was planning to slide slowly down the cliff by hooking the rope under her thigh, across her body, and over the opposite shoulder. Her hands could release the rope a little at a time to control the speed of her descent.

After wrapping her hands with cloth to protect her palms, she began her downward trip. It turned out to be far from easy. She kept bumping into tiny bushes and boulders and had to move around them. As the rope slid across her body, she inched down a little at a time. She kicked up a lot of dry soil, which filled the air and made it harder to breathe. To top it off, about fifty feet from the ground, she ran out of rope.

Dangling five stories above the ground, she looked around for some ideas. The only things within reach were small bushes. She tugged on the row of bushes above and below her. They seemed well rooted despite the dry soil. Using the bushes below as a step and holding on to the overhead bushes for balance, Joon let go of the rope. She could feel it sliding past her thigh and shoulder. Then she grabbed hold of it again and pulled it down from the tree above. She relooped it around the base of a nearby bush. Then, holding her breath, she continued her downward slide.

Thirty feet from the ground, she felt a slight drop, and she knew the roots of the bush were coming loose. She quickened her pace and managed to travel twenty more feet before the bush gave way and she plunged ten feet to the ground. Keeping her knees bent, Joon landed on her feet and tumbled to the side. Other than a racing heart and many scrapes, she was fine.

The winds continued to shower smoldering coals around her as she moved through the smoke-filled woods. The smoke was making it difficult to breathe. Joon wet a bandanna with water from her canteen and tied it around her mouth. She wanted to head toward Norris, the closest park village, but the fires seemed to have cut off all of its approaches. She decided to head for the Lake Yellowstone Hotel, although it was farther away. She thought that it would be safe there. She thought that she could make it.

With her compass and map, Joon plotted out the most direct course. She could not afford to wander. It was possible to stay ahead of the fire as long as the wind maintained its present speed. Joon's heart pumped with fearful excitement.

About an hour later, she noticed a stream of smoke swirling up into the sky to the south. She climbed a nearby tree and peered through her binoculars. A violent fire similar to the one at Inspiration Point was raging toward her in the distance.

She looked to the west and found a solid streak of fire there as well. The fire now surrounded her on three sides. At any moment, she could find herself enclosed by a wall of flames without a way out. Joon had to think of a fast escape. Her only choice was to head east—and fast!

The sun was setting, and she knew that she would have to walk through the night to keep ahead of the flames. She unpacked her flashlight and snacked on some beef jerky as she pushed her stiff, tired legs almost to their limit. As the sunlight disappeared, a slim flashlight beam was her only company through the dark woods.

She kept a steady pace until a violent rustling of leaves startled her. Switching off her flashlight, she stood still and listened for clues. With squinting eyes, she tried to see what was around her. Then, about twenty feet away from her, Joon recognized the outline of a bear.

She spotted an easy tree to climb but decided not to go for it yet. The tree might not be safe. Also, any sudden movement would only attract the bear's attention. As the bear inched closer to her, she reminded herself to keep calm. Her best chance was to count on the animal's poor eyesight.

The bear had not yet picked up her scent, but it was getting closer by the minute. Joon was about to rush up a tree when the bear unexpectedly lumbered off in the opposite direction. She watched it go and, for the first time in five minutes, took a full breath.

Fortunately, this was the only obstacle during her night journey, other than fatigue and sore feet. She kept checking behind her, but the fire seemed to have taken a different route.

Just before sunrise, she reached the Lake Yellowstone Hotel. It would offer the first hot meal and warm bed that she had had in days. But before eating or sleeping, she called her family. They told her that they had been horribly worried and were thrilled that she was safe.

Joon stayed in the hotel until the great fires subsided. Each day, acre after acre was consumed by the blaze. It was a painful sight for her to witness. She loved the forest and hated to see it destroyed.

The moment that the fires were under control, she jumped back into her hiking gear and took off to the trails. Huge sections of wooded areas were still smoking. Her favorite trail stood bare and black.

Sitting at the edge of Firehole River, Joon felt weak. Much of Yellowstone's beauty had been reduced to ashes. She felt as if she had lost a dear friend.

Suddenly, a group of elk began to graze just a few feet away from her on a small patch of unburned meadow. Joon was amazed by their calm manner. They didn't seem bothered by the latest event. It was all a part of life for them. They had a simple focus. They were just going to eat what they could and move on.

For the first time, Joon saw a certain beauty in her scorched surroundings. She reached down and scooped up a handful of earth. This mixture of burned leaves and bark would renew itself. Soon, young plants would begin to grow here. All of it was part of the natural cycle of life.

READING FOR UNDERSTANDING

1. What did Joon see in the distance when she first stopped at Inspiration Point?

2. Why do you think that she reacted as she did to what she saw?

3. How did her reaction change when she got her second view of the same thing?

4. Why did she return to Inspiration Point?

5. How did Joon get down the side of the plateau at Inspiration Point?

6. Suggest several reasons why Joon decided that climbing a tree to escape the bear might not be safe.

7. Does the writer of this story make any basic points about nature? What are they?

RESPONDING TO THE STORY

Joon couldn't resist getting a closer look at the fire. Because she gave in to this urge, she almost was trapped. Have you ever gotten yourself into a dangerous or difficult situation because you couldn't resist doing something? What was it, and what happened?

REVIEWING VOCABULARY

The following sentences are based on the story. Decide which of the words following the sentences best fits each blank. Write your answers on a separate sheet of paper.

1. This story took place during a _____ hike in Yellowstone National Park.

2. During the hike, a serious fire became a dangerous _____ to Joon.

3. Joon was extremely frightened by the bear that _____ by in the woods.

4. Because she was an experienced climber, she knew how to _____ safely down the edge of a cliff.

5. Even in the _____ surroundings, Joon saw beauty.

Words: *solitary, lumbered, rappel, scorched, obstacle*

THINKING CRITICALLY

1. When Joon rappelled down the cliff, she barely made it. Fortunately, she was an experienced climber and knew what to do. Describe what might happen to an inexperienced climber in the same situation.

2. Joon's family was thrilled that she was safe. But before she called, they had been very worried. What might they have said to her on the telephone about the risks that she took?

3. In what way is a destructive forest fire part of the natural cycle of life? Was Joon right in finally coming to accept it and in seeing a certain beauty in it? Explain.

THE TRIANGLE FIRE

Cecilia Rubino Lucas

"FIRE!" *The following story is based on an event that really happened. On March 25, 1911, nearly 150 garment workers were killed when a terrible fire swept through the Triangle Shirtwaist Company in New York City.*

There was no warning or protection for most of the workers. In the early 1900s, fire alarms and sprinklers were not required in buildings as they are today. Most of today's laws enforcing safety precautions and procedures had not yet been passed.

Most of the garment workers of those days were young immigrant women. Working conditions were terrible, but these were the only jobs that these women could find. Some factory owners treated their workers badly. They were underpaid, and they worked for ten hours a day under conditions that would be considered unacceptable today. Perhaps the most horrible fact about the Triangle Fire was that when the panicked workers tried to escape, they found that the exit doors had been locked—by their own supervisors.

VOCABULARY WORDS

cavernous (KAV-uhr-nuhs) big and hollow like a cave
❖ The *cavernous* civic center held more than 8,000 people.

smoldered (SMOHL-duhrd) burned and smoked without flames
❖ The charcoal *smoldered* in the grill as we cooked steaks.

ignited (ihg-NYT-uhd) set on fire
❖ The fire *ignited* the pile of old newspapers.

engulfed (ehn-GULFD) swallowed up
❖ Before the fire department could reach the warehouse, the building was *engulfed* in flames.

inferno (ihn-FER-noh) place full of fire or great heat
❖ We could only pray that no one was trapped inside the blazing *inferno*.

intense (ihn-TEHNS) very strong
❖ The heat from the fire was so *intense* that the police ordered the crowds to stand back.

singe (SIHNJ) burn a little at the ends
❖ Don't let that candle *singe* your hair.

soot (SOOT) black substance made up of carbon from fire
❖ You should regularly clean out the *soot* that builds up in your chimney.

KEY WORD

Signorina (see-nyah-REE-nah) Italian for "Miss"
❖ Dr. Corelli tipped his hat and greeted Teresa cheerfully, "Good day, *Signorina!*"

Fannie Venturella worked six days a week, but today was Saturday. On Saturdays, the Triangle Shirtwaist Factory closed up early. And Saturday was payday, too. Fannie straightened her back and switched off her sewing machine. She picked up the brown envelope from her worktable. Anna Gullo, the forewoman on the ninth floor, had passed out pay envelopes a few moments before, but Fannie hadn't dared to stop working. She quickly glanced inside: $5.50. Her first week's pay for operating her own machine!

It didn't seem like much for sixty hours of bending over a sewing machine. All day, every day, she stitched sleeve after sleeve into fashionable women's shirts. Now, she breathed a sigh of relief. At least this check was a step in the right direction. It was her first check in four long weeks. There was no pay for the period that it took her to learn on this new machine. Still, it was an opportunity that could not be passed up. Before that, she had sewed buttons all day on the eighth floor for only three dollars a week. Her sister, Rose, was still slaving away down there. Rose was only fourteen. Fannie had just turned sixteen.

Fannie got her chance to work at a sewing machine when her Aunt Rita bought the forewoman a pair of fur gloves for Christmas. A couple of months later, Fannie was promoted. Aunt Rose worked in another section of the cavernous ninth floor. But Fannie never got a chance to talk to her or even see her until the ten-hour work day was over.

Fannie rubbed her eyes. She was dizzy. That's how exhausted she was. Staring at tiny stitches all day turned your vision into a blur by the last hour. Fannie put one arm on her sewing table to steady herself.

Maybe the dizzy spell was just from the closeness of the room. So many workers were packed into this one room that sometimes it felt like there was no air to breathe. Even so, nobody dared to complain.

At the Triangle Shirtwaist Factory, the bosses held all the cards. Most of the young women who worked there were from Italian or Jewish immigrant families. They didn't have the money to go to school, and there weren't that many kinds of jobs open to them. If a worker complained, she was sent packing and was replaced immediately with a new worker.

The large sweatshop, which vibrated all day with the hum of 240 sewing machines, was now filled with the chatter of young women, as they got up from their work stations. Fannie dropped the last shirt that she'd been stitching into the wicker basket at her feet.

Then she remembered the damaged blouse. She looked up quickly. Anna Gullo, the forewoman, was across the room. Fannie had gotten so tired an hour before that she'd almost sewed one of her fingers right into the seam of the blouse. To Fannie's great relief, the needle of the machine didn't break. But it pierced her skin enough to bleed. And though she quickly band-aged it with a scrap of material, the blouse that she was working on was ruined. Fannie was too embarrassed to say anything. Employees usually paid for damaged work, and she couldn't afford it. What was she going to do with the bloody shirt?

She'd have to clean it to get rid of it. But all the doors on her floor were locked to prevent theft. The workers were herded through a single exit at the end of the working day. All their bags were checked. She didn't dare try to walk out with the blouse.

Nervously, Fannie bent down and stuffed the stained shirt under her work basket. She sprang up and headed for the cloak room at the back of the shop. Aunt Rita would know what to do. Fannie found her, with her coat already on, in the crowded dressing room.

Aunt Rita looked exhausted, but there was a twinkle in her eyes. "You better hurry along, Signorina!" she said. She winked at Fannie as she pinned a broad hat on top of her twisted knot of black hair. "We've got a few stops to make on our way home tonight, remember." Rita had promised to take her nieces shopping that evening. It was almost Easter. The two girls wanted to send chocolates, along with the few dollars they'd saved, as a surprise to their Mama and Papa back in Italy. Fannie thought about how happy her parents would be to get the Easter gift. They would take the chocolates as a sign that the girls were doing well and had enough money to buy presents. Mama hadn't wanted to let them come to the United States. But Aunt Rita had written, saying that the girls could stay in her front room on Elizabeth Street and that she was sure to get them a job.

"Auntie Rita, I . . ." Suddenly, as Fannie leaned towards her aunt, the chatter of the young women around her was pierced by a terrified scream.

"FIRE! LOOK! OUT THE WINDOW!"

Without warning, thick smoke started pouring into the crowded cloak room. A fire had started on the floor below them fifteen minutes earlier. It smoldered undetected in the mountains of scrap material under the shirt cutters' long, wooden tables. Then it ignited the racks of flimsy paper patterns that swung over the cutters' heads. Suddenly, the entire eighth floor was engulfed in flames.

In those days, there was no fire alarm system. There was no sprinkler system, either! No one had had time to warn the 260 people on the floor above about the raging inferno. By the time that Rita grabbed Fannie's arm and dragged her back out into the shop, flames were leaping in through the windows along Washington Place. Fannie could hear women crying out in Italian and Yiddish. Some of the women froze at their machines, too frightened to move. Others fainted and were trampled by other terrified young women trying to squeeze their way through the narrow aisles between the sewing tables.

Rita rushed Fannie to the staircase on the Washington Street side. But the door was locked as usual! Women were pounding on it, screaming. Another crowd crushed toward the elevators, but none was coming up. Rita shouted at Fannie to follow her, but Fannie got lost in the confusion. Smoke was billowing in from everywhere. The wicker baskets of material, wooden chairs, and the well-oiled sewing machines were catching fire all around her.

Fannie scrambled up onto one of the wooden tables and began to leap from table to table across the room. There was a staircase on the Greene Street side. She had to get down the stairs. Rose was downstairs! In the fire! She had to get Rose!

When she reached the Greene Street stairs, Fannie found the entrance cut off by a wall of flame. She couldn't get through because the heat was too intense. She started for the windows. Women were climbing out and standing on the ledges, their long skirts catching on fire. But the thought of falling from a window was even more terrifying than the flames. She'd always been afraid of heights. Fannie ran back into the center of the shop, slapping frantically at her own hair as the ends started to singe. She grabbed a roll of thin, white material and wrapped it around and around herself until all that was showing was her eyes.

Desperately, she rushed through the wall of flames into the Greene Street stairwell. She couldn't go down. The flames were too dense. Her skirts were catching on fire. Suddenly, Fannie heard a voice calling, "TO THE ROOF, THE ROOF!" She raced up the stairs, twisting and turning, peeling off the burning material as she ran. She got past the tenth floor and burst onto the roof, leaving the material burning in a ribbon of fire behind her. A young woman whom she'd never seen before helped her beat out the flames on her skirt. Then they saw some law students standing on the roof of the university building that was next to the factory. They ran toward the young men and were lifted to safety.

When Fannie finally got down to the street, she called out wildly for her sister: "ROSE? ROSE? ROSE!"

Then she saw a horrible sight. Bodies were lying on the sidewalks. Young women were jumping from the burning building like torches being thrown from the windows. Fannie sat down on the sidewalk, weeping in disbelief. Snow was beginning to fall. A man came over and looked into her face. He took a handkerchief and wiped the soot from her cheeks.

"I thought you were my sister," he said, as he put his coat around her shoulders.

Fannie never learned the man's name. As she looked around, she caught sight of her Aunt Rita. Rita was looking frantically for her nieces.

When Fannie's eyes met Rita's, her aunt gave a terrible cry of happiness and relief. Together they looked for Rose. But Rose had not been so lucky. She was among the hundreds who died in the sweatshop fire that day.

Neither Rita nor Fannie ever forgot that horrible day or the last time that they saw Rose alive on the eighth floor. They did not return to the Triangle Shirtwaist Factory. They took other jobs that were not much better. They also became involved in a growing movement to improve working conditions. Several years later, new laws were passed to protect sweatshop workers against fire, low pay, and unhealthy working conditions. By that time, Rita and Fannie no longer had to work in sweatshops. They had saved what little money they had to open their own dress shop on Elizabeth Street. The shop was called "Rose's."

READING FOR UNDERSTANDING

1. The story takes place in a factory in **(a)** New York **(b)** South Carolina **(c)** San Francisco.

2. Fannie was glad that the needle of her machine did not break because **(a)** she didn't want to pay for a new one **(b)** the needle belonged to her **(c)** needles were hard to find at the time.

3. When the fire broke out, Fannie had been worrying about **(a)** the danger of fire **(b)** shopping with Rita **(c)** a damaged blouse.

4. During the fire, Fannie desperately tried **(a)** to work the sprinkler system **(b)** to call Rita **(c)** to save Rose.

5. Rita and Fannie named their dress shop "Rose's" because **(a)** they thought that such a name would attract customers **(b)** they hoped Rose would be found alive **(c)** they wanted to honor Rose's memory.

RESPONDING TO THE STORY

The tragedy of the Triangle Fire might have been prevented. There should have been an alarm system. The doors should not have been locked. How do these details affect how you responded to the story? Explain in a paragraph.

REVIEWING VOCABULARY

The following sentences are based on the story. Decide which of the words following the sentences best fits each blank. Write your answers on a separate sheet of paper.

1. Aunt Rita worked in another section of the building's _____ ninth floor.
2. The fire rapidly _____ the racks of paper patterns.
3. The entire eighth floor was _____ in flames.
4. The heat was so _____ that Fannie couldn't get through.
5. A man used his handkerchief to wipe the _____ from Fannie's cheeks.
6. No one warned the workers on the ninth floor of the _____ raging on the level below them.

Words: *engulfed, soot, cavernous, ignited, inferno, intense*

THINKING CRITICALLY

1. As you learned from the story, the word *sweatshop* was used to describe factories like the Triangle Shirtwaist Factory. Explain why this word is appropriate.
2. What do the details about the damaged blouse tell you about the rules and conditions of work at Triangle? Do you think that working conditions are still very difficult for some people? Explain.
3. Once she knew that fire had broken out, Fannie faced a painful conflict. What was this conflict? How might you have handled it if you had been in Fannie's position?

Unit 3
WAVES OF PANIC

TOO MUCH ROOM
Dina Anastasio

Imagine being a passenger on the newest, largest ocean liner of your time. This was true for a young woman and her brother when they boarded the Titanic *on its first voyage in April 1912. The ship was equipped with all the latest navigating equipment. The engineers who designed the* Titanic *called it "unsinkable." The ship was traveling from England to New York.*

Excitement soon turned to panic, though, when the boat collided with an iceberg. People refused to believe that the unsinkable ship was sinking.

While the Titanic *sank, people reacted differently. Some people tried to help as many people as they could. Others were too frightened to help. This story tells how a young woman and her brother faced this terrifying event.*

VOCABULARY WORDS

dislodged (dihs-LAHJD) forced out of a place
❖ She kept coughing until the food was *dislodged* from her throat.

listing (LIHS-tihng) tilting to one side
❖ The boat was *listing* because everyone crowded to one side to see the whale.

midst (MIHDST) middle
❖ In the *midst* of the crowded room, I saw my boyfriend.

steward (STOO-uhrd) person who looks after the passengers on a ship
❖ He asked the *steward* what time lunch would be served.

stern (STUHRN) rear part of a ship
❖ We stood at the *stern* and watched the harbor as we sailed away.

bow (bow) front part of a ship
❖ The captain stood at the *bow* of the ship.

huddled (HUD-uhld) crowded close together
❖ They *huddled* together to keep warm.

oarlocks (OWR-lahks) device used for holding the oars in place in rowing or steering
❖ Before they started out rowing, they put the oars in the *oarlocks*.

slackened (SLAK-uhnd) made or became less strong
❖ The rain *slackened* after an hour.

coincidentally (koh-ihn-suh-DEHN-tuhl-lee) occurring by chance at the same time
❖ They met *coincidentally* while they were waiting for the same train.

 **E**mma Davidson was a light sleeper. The squeak of a mouse or the softest footstep would disturb her sleep.

On this particular night, it was her trunk that woke her. For some unknown reason, the trunk skidded across the floor and crashed into the wall on the other side of the cabin.

"What's that noise?" Emma asked, sitting up in her bed. It took her a moment to remember that she was on a huge ocean liner. The *Titanic* was taking her from her home in England to the United States.

"What noise?" her brother Ben asked from the bunk below hers.

"That THUMP. Didn't you hear it?"

Before Ben had a chance to answer, they heard another crash. Emma flipped on the light. Her mother's bunk was empty.

"Mum's not back from dinner," she said nervously.

Suddenly, a chair dislodged itself and slid across the floor. Ben sat up and looked at his sister with wide, frightened eyes.

"What's going on?" he whispered.

At eighteen, Emma was supposed to know what to say to her fourteen-year-old brother. But she couldn't think of anything at all. The great *Titanic* was listing badly, and it seemed to be getting worse by the minute.

Emma grabbed her coat and threw it over her nightgown. Then she tossed Ben his jacket and pulled him out of bed and out of the cabin. Outside in the long, narrow hallway, the lights were flickering on and off.

"I'm scared, Emma," Ben said.

Far ahead, someone was screaming. Emma held Ben's hand tightly as they slid along the wall. She was scared too, but she didn't want Ben to know.

"Where's Mum?" asked Ben. He was trying hard not to panic.

"We'll find her," Emma answered, trying to sound confident. But she wasn't so sure. The main hallway was crowded with anxious people, and she didn't see her mother anywhere.

Emma pulled Ben through the crowd and stopped. She could hardly believe it, but someone was calling her name in the midst of this madness.

"We're here!" Emma responded loudly. "Over here!"

Emma's favorite steward heard her and rushed over. "Your mother couldn't get to you," he explained. "I promised her that I'd get you and your brother into a lifeboat. She had to get into one immediately because she was already on deck."

Emma thanked the steward warmly. This man had been so kind to her family during the whole voyage. Then she turned to her brother. Emma squeezed Ben's hand hard. She understood what the steward meant, but she wondered if Ben did. The *Titanic* was sinking!

Holding Ben's hand, she followed the steward up the staircase to the boat deck. Together, they walked to the railing and looked down into the rough, black water. Shadowy lifeboats dipped in and out of the large, dark waves.

"Quick!" the steward told them. "Jump into that one." Many people needed the steward's help at the other side of the deck. He hurried away, leaving Emma and Ben alone.

From what they could see, it was the last lifeboat, and it was still almost empty. Only five people were huddled together at the stern, but Emma couldn't make out their faces.

"Where is everybody?" Ben asked. "Why don't they fill the boat?"

The lifeboat was about to be lowered, but Emma and Ben didn't want to go yet. They wanted to help fill it first. Holding Ben's hand tightly, Emma raced across the deck, saw an old woman, and helped her to the lifeboat. She called for others, but no one came to this side of the deck. Except for Emma and Ben, the deck was empty.

"Emma, hurry!" Ben cried. "The boat's going!"

Emma swung around and stared at the almost-empty lifeboat. It was swinging out over the water. In a minute, it would be lowered into the waves. They raced toward it and climbed in together. Crouching, they scrambled toward the bow.

The support chains creaked, as the lifeboat was lowered slowly to the sea. The children could see and hear people screaming from each of the *Titanic*'s other decks. There was no way to stop the lifeboat. There was no way to move it closer to the inhabited decks on the sinking ship. There was no way to save those terrified people.

The lifeboat hit the water with a THUD. Then it rocked from side to side as it was released and set free in the waves.

"Get away from the ship!" someone shouted from above. "Row! Row for your lives, or the ship will take you down with it when it sinks!"

Emma and Ben peered through the darkness at their fellow passengers.

"We have to row!" Emma called.

But no one answered. All of the others were huddled fearfully at the other end under blankets and coats.

"Quick!" Emma pleaded. "Please, someone help us find the oars."

"We're too scared," a shaky voice replied. "Besides, we don't know how to row a boat."

92

Emma rubbed her eyes and studied the people in the boat. It was true. None of the people in the boat had the slightest idea of what to do. None of them would be able to help.

Ben poked her and pointed toward the giant gray ship beside them. It was listing badly now, and if it went down, it would suck them under with it! They had to get away fast!

"Hurry and get the oars, Ben!" Emma said.

Ben crawled around until he found both oars. Then he placed them in the oarlocks and sat in the middle seat. Both Ben and Emma had taken rowing lessons last summer.

"I'll row first," he said.

Emma came and sat beside him. "You can't do it alone," she said. "Try taking one oar, and I'll take the other."

Above them, the frightened crowd screamed louder as the lights flickered all over the massive ship.

The huge ship was sinking fast! Flares were being shot off on the bow. Maybe, if there were another ship nearby, help would come in time.

"Row, Ben," Emma called. "Row when I say *three*. Okay, one, two, THREE!"

They pulled together, and the lifeboat inched away from the ship.

"One, two, THREE!" The lifeboat moved another few inches.

Emma was bigger and stronger than Ben, and if she pulled with all her strength, the lifeboat would go around in circles. So she slackened her rowing and pulled lightly. The lifeboat moved slowly away from the great sinking ship.

When they were finally a distance away, Emma and Ben raised their oars and watched as the bow of the

93

giant liner slipped below the water. Emma closed her eyes. It was too awful to watch it disappear. When, at last, she opened them, the ship was gone. Only the stars remained shining brightly overhead.

The people in the other lifeboats were silent. Then, the water came alive with the sounds of their cries.

"Save the people in the water!" they shouted. "Over there! On your left!"

"Row, Ben, row!" Emma directed. "We have to find as many as we can!"

Emma and Ben rowed through the night. By morning, the lifeboat was crowded. Two of the survivors were rowing now, as Emma and Ben rested.

When the rescue ship finally arrived, everyone was wet and hungry. Emma and Ben climbed up the ship's ladder carefully and then fell into the arms of the ship's doctor.

"Is our mother here?" Ben asked.

The doctor wrote down their names. Coincidentally, he had seen their mother just a few moments before. He instantly recognized the names, and he reassured the young people. Then he provided them with dry clothes and led them into the dining room. When they had their food, he went to search for their mother.

A few minutes later the doctor had the satisfaction of bringing the family all together. When their mother had stopped crying, she said: "I met some people who say you saved their lives. They say that you found them in the water."

Emma smiled and shrugged. "We had room in the lifeboat. In fact, we had much too much room!"

READING FOR UNDERSTANDING

1. Emma woke up because she heard **(a)** a mouse **(b)** a thump **(c)** her brother crying.

2. Emma was traveling **(a)** from the United States to England **(b)** from England to the United States **(c)** from England to Iceland.

3. Emma understood that the boat was sinking when **(a)** her shoe slid across the floor **(b)** their mother was not in her bunk **(c)** the steward mentioned the lifeboat.

4. Emma was someone who **(a)** panics **(b)** takes charge **(c)** behaves selfishly.

5. When Emma said that the lifeboat had "much too much room", she meant that **(a)** it was too big to row easily **(b)** its space should have been filled with more rescued people **(c)** it should have had her mother on it.

6. By the end of the story, Emma wished that **(a)** they had never taken this trip **(b)** she had been with her mother **(c)** she could have saved more people.

RESPONDING TO THE STORY

Sometimes we can't imagine how we would react in a certain situation. Emma probably didn't think of herself as a heroine before that fateful night. Have you ever been in a situation where you reacted in a surprising way? Describe it in a paragraph. What did you learn about yourself?

REVIEWING VOCABULARY

Match each word on the left with the correct definition on the right.

1. bow	**a.** tilting to one side
2. coincidentally	**b.** front part of a ship
3. dislodged	**c.** forced out of a place
4. huddled	**d.** rear part of a ship
5. listing	**e.** crowded close together
6. midst	**f.** occurring by chance at the same time
7. slackened	**g.** middle
8. stern	**h.** made or became less strong
9. steward	**i.** person who looks after passengers on a ship
10. oarlocks	**j.** device that holds oars in place

THINKING CRITICALLY

1. Instead of immediately jumping into the lifeboat, Emma and Ben first helped an old lady in. Why do you think such a brave act was worth the risk for them?

2. Why do you think that the other people in the lifeboat with Emma and Ben did not want to row? Suggest some reasons in addition to the one that they gave.

3. Presently, very few people cross the Atlantic Ocean by ship. Airplanes have taken the place of ocean liners. What kinds of heroism could people show in an airplane during a similar tragedy?

AND NOT A DROP TO DRINK

Brenda Lane Richardson

The title of this story was inspired by the famous poem, "The Rime of the Ancient Mariner," by Samuel Taylor Coleridge. The poem tells the tale of an old seaman whose ship becomes cursed when he shoots a bird. Suddenly, the winds die down, and the ship is stranded. The crew fear that they will die of thirst in the middle of the ocean. In the poem, they cry out, "Water, water, everywhere, / Nor any drop to drink." For the sailors, the water is an enemy. For LaShanda, the main character in "And Not a Drop to Drink," water also is the enemy.

LaShanda and her family live in St. Charles, Missouri. It is one of the river towns in the Midwest that was devastated by floods during the summer of 1993. St. Charles is very near the junction of the Mississippi and Missouri rivers. For families like LaShanda's, whose houses were in low-lying areas, the situation was critical. Flood waters threatened to swallow them up, along with everything they owned.

Would you be able to act quickly and sensibly in an emergency? The pressure to do the right thing in a crisis is great enough if you're alone. It's even greater when you are responsible for young children, as LaShanda is in this story. Read on to see how she faces this crisis.

VOCABULARY WORDS

concerns (kuhn-SERNZ) worries
❖ When we saw how badly she was hurt, we quickly forgot our own *concerns*.

static (STAT-ihk) electrical interference
❖ The *static* on the telephone line interrupted our conversation.

advising (ad-VYZ-ihng) informing
❖ Cabinet members were *advising* the president during the recent crisis.

evacuation (ee-vak-yoo-AY-shuhn) emergency departure
❖ During the storm, the police helped with the *evacuation* of townspeople.

muffled (MUF-uhld) partly deadened
❖ The heavy snowfall *muffled* the noise of city traffic for an entire day.

wade (WAYD) walk through shallow water
❖ We like to *wade* in the pool.

embrace (em-BRAYS) hug
❖ Helen ran to meet her cousin and gave him an affectionate *embrace*.

"**H**old on a minute." LaShanda put the telephone under her arm and screamed to the children upstairs: "Stop fighting. I'll be off in two more minutes, then you'll get your reward."

LaShanda's two-year-old sister, Jackie, and her five year-old brother, Kenny, cheered. LaShanda promised hot chocolate with whipped cream and chocolate chips if they cleaned their room. While they were cleaning, she wanted to talk with her best friend about that new boy in town. LaShanda had hoped to meet him at the dance last night, but the rainstorm had shut down her town, St. Charles, Missouri.

As LaShanda put the telephone back to her ear, she glanced again toward the large picture window, which was covered by drapes, and listened to the rain beating against the glass. She shivered, thinking that she'd be glad when her parents returned from getting groceries. Then she quickly forgot her concerns.

"Okay, girl, so tell me everything." LaShanda was greeted with silence. "Hello, hello, where are you?" She held on, thinking that her friend had put the telephone down for a minute. Finally, the recorded voice of an operator said: "If you'd like to make a call, please hang up and dial again. If you need help, please hang up and dial your operator."

LaShanda frowned. "I need help all right. Help me get the rundown on that new guy." All that she could get from the telephone now was static. Things had set-tled down upstairs, so LaShanda figured that she owed it to herself to tune into her favorite television soap opera. She'd promised her mother that she would play with the kids, but this was different, wasn't it? How many times in life would she be this lucky? No mother to scold her about watching too many soaps, and the kids actually behaving.

Grabbing a bag of potato chips and easing herself onto the sofa, LaShanda imagined Mama saying: "No shoes on the couch. I've told you a million times to take your shoes off before you get on my white couch!" LaShanda wasn't worried. The large picture window was right in front of her. She figured that she could keep getting up, lift the drapes, and check for the car. Before her parents were even in the driveway, she'd be off the couch and upstairs with the kids.

Remote control in hand, she settled into the cushions. To her disgust, her show had been interrupted by the news. The television stations were always doing that. Didn't they realize that she and probably a trillion other people didn't even care about the news?

She flicked through every station and was stunned to see the same kinds of pictures on every channel: firefighters helping elderly people out of their homes, and people loading furniture and suitcases into cars. The scene faded to a reporter saying: "We repeat. If you live in a lowland area, leave your home immediately. Police are advising evacuation."

LaShanda's heart skipped a beat. She ran to the picture window, hoping to see her parents' car. Then she screamed. The yard looked like a muddy swimming pool. The water was up to the top step.

The sounds of little feet came banging down the stairs. "LaShanda, why did you scream?" Kenny asked. He was small for his age, with large round eyes and close-cut hair. Jackie, still in her footed pajamas, hugged her teddy bear in her arms and sucked a thumb, as they waited for LaShanda's answer.

LaShanda played at looking calm. "How else am I going to get you downstairs?" The children looked relieved. LaShanda quickly thought of a plan. "We're going to play a game."

"No! I want chocolate now!" Kenny demanded.

"Okay, we'll take the chocolate with us," LaShanda said. She grabbed the backpack that she used like a purse, and, holding the children's hands, pulled them into the kitchen. "I'm putting the milk in here." She tried stuffing an unopened carton into her bag, but her bag was full of music magazines, an old hat, and candy and gum wrappers. All this she dumped onto the floor.

"Ooh," Kenny said, "Mama's gonna get you."

"Get the chocolate, Kenny." LaShanda's heart pounded as she raced to get milk, towels, cereal, cans of cola, and pretzels.

"Game, game," repeated Jackie, who was seated on a stool.

"Yes," said LaShanda, creating her plan as she spoke. "The game is that I'll put Jackie on my back, and she carries the backpack on her back, and then we see who can get onto the roof the fastest."

Kenny was out of the kitchen even before LaShanda could lift Jackie onto her back. "Cocoa!" Jackie screamed. Kenny had left the chocolate on the counter-top. LaShanda didn't care about the chocolate. She wanted to get onto the roof before the water began streaming under the door. Jackie kept insisting, kicking LaShanda's sides like a rider on a horse. LaShanda turned back into the kitchen, reached for the cocoa, and took off after her brother.

"Kenny, Kenny!" LaShanda yelled, as she climbed the stairs. Except for the rain pounding on the windows, the house was silent. Silent, LaShanda thought, the way the telephone had been when she'd tried to pick up on her conversation with her friend. LaShanda hoped that her parents and friends were okay.

She rounded a corner and moved quickly toward the closet that hid the dusty old stairs to the roof. When she pulled the door open, Kenny jumped out screaming. LaShanda began crying. Kenny looked shocked. As she sobbed, LaShanda said, "Don't ever do that to me again!" Kenny seemed to be fighting back giggles.

His laughter didn't last for long. As LaShanda pulled open the door to the roof and helped the children out, they saw for miles around them that water was everywhere. Now Kenny was crying too. Jackie, still on LaShanda's back, squeezed her sister's neck so hard, LaShanda started to choke.

If LaShanda had thought that the roof would make her feel safer, she'd been mistaken. Now they could see that only a mile away, the roofs of some houses were

covered by water. "That can happen to us," she thought, and looked up, hoping to see a helicopter. It occurred to her that the idea of being rescued was the sort of thing that she'd seen on a soap opera. In real life, she thought, I'm the one who's going to have to figure out how to save us. The driving rain muffled her sobs and the panicked cries of Kenny and Jackie. But it was time to act.

LaShanda held the attic door open. Kenny scrambled back in and then climbed down the stairs. LaShanda, with Jackie in her arms, followed. LaShanda closed the attic door behind her. The house was as silent as a tomb. She lowered her voice. "Okay, Kenny, I finally fooled you, didn't I?" she asked. "You were really scared there for a moment, weren't you?"

The boy watched her carefully, checking to see if LaShanda was joking. She made her smile stretch wider. Kenny wiped an arm across his tear-stained face as LaShanda said, "Now, here's the rest of the game. We're going to wade through the water outside, and this time we don't care how much mud we get on us." LaShanda felt like Jackie's weight was breaking her shoulders, but she refused to let her little sister down.

"Kenny, the other part of the game is that you must hold onto my hand and you can't let go, no matter what. Promise?" He nodded his head uncertainly.

The front door wouldn't open. It had been swollen shut by the water. LaShanda wanted to break the picture window, but worried the glass might hurt one of the children. Forcing open another window, she lowered herself outside with Jackie still on her back, and then waited for Kenny. After he climbed out the window, LaShanda saw that the water was up to his waist.

As she passed one neighbor's house after another, LaShanda realized that this was more than just rain.

The Mississippi River must have flooded. Her plan was to move toward Potter's Hill. It was the highest spot in the neighborhood. It was only a block away, but now it seemed so far.

LaShanda saw the hill. She'd been right. There were lots of people waiting there. She could barely see through the rain and her own tears. Suddenly, a big arm covered by the sleeves of a raincoat reached out toward her. Suddenly, Jackie was off her back. It was her father, lifting both Kenny and Jackie. "Oh, Daddy," she cried. "Where is Mommy?" Before she could say another word, she felt her mother's embrace and was pulled toward high land.

By the time that LaShanda and her family were on the top of the hill, she realized that they would all be okay. Her mother held her face between her hands. Now it was her mother who was crying. "You did fine, honey. The police wouldn't let us go down there. We were trying to get to you. But you know what? I knew you'd do the right thing. . . . You just remind me of that the next time I fuss about something."

LaShanda put her head on her mother's chest. Though they were all wet and muddy, it didn't matter.

READING FOR UNDERSTANDING

The following paragraph summarizes the story. Decide which of the words below the paragraph best fits in each blank. Write your answers on a separate sheet of paper.

LaShanda sent her younger **(1)**_____ and sister to clean their **(2)**_____. When her **(3)**_____ went dead, she watched television. Frightened by news reports about the storm, she looked out the **(4)**_____. She **(5)**_____ when she saw water in the yard. LaShanda pretended to be **(6)**_____, as she told the younger children that they were going to play a new **(7)**_____. Her plan was to fill a **(8)**_____ with supplies and climb up to the **(9)**_____. LaShanda helped the children up the old **(10)**_____. But, when she saw roofs covered by **(11)**_____, LaShanda took the children back down. She told them to **(12)**_____ through the yard. The front **(13)**_____ was swollen shut, so LaShanda forced open a window. She realized that the Mississippi River must have **(14)**_____. She led the children to Potter's Hill, the **(15)**_____ spot nearby.

Words: *game, calm, water, backpack, brother, stairs, highest, screamed, room, wade, flooded, window, telephone, door, roof*

RESPONDING TO THE STORY

Assume that you are LaShanda's father or mother. In a diary entry written about a week after the storm, describe how you feel about your daughter's actions.

REVIEWING VOCABULARY

1. Sound is *muffled* if it is **(a)** clear **(b)** loud **(c)** deadened.
2. In an *evacuation*, people **(a)** meet **(b)** arrive **(c)** leave.
3. When parents are *advising* their children, they are **(a)** punishing them **(b)** giving them suggestions **(c)** rewarding them.
4. *Static* on a telephone line **(a)** raises volume **(b)** interferes with reception **(c)** makes the line go dead.
5. When Isabel told us of her *concerns*, we understood her **(a)** worries **(b)** memories **(c)** jokes.
6. Her *embrace* was a **(a)** poke **(b)** hug **(c)** handshake.
7. We *wade* in water when it is **(a)** deep **(b)** cold **(c)** shallow.

THINKING CRITICALLY

1. How were LaShanda's outlook on life and her behavior typical for a girl her age?
2. What is your opinion of people who have no interest in the news? Why do you think they aren't interested?
3. From hints in the story, how would you describe LaShanda's relationship with her mother before the storm? How had the relationship changed by the end of the story?
4. Why did LaShanda put on an act? What did her pretending for the children's sake tell you about her character?
5. Do you agree with LaShanda's mother that LaShanda acted properly during the storm? Would you have acted differently? If so, how?

EARTH AND AIR, FIRE AND WATER

Carroll Moulton

The characters in this story live by means of the water, air, and earth around them. The water supplies the fish that they eat. The air powers the sails that drive their boats. The earth grows the rice plants that they use as food. They farm and fish on a beautiful South Pacific island. For hundreds of years, they have been living in this same simple way.

Then one day, fire is added to the water, air, and earth. Everything suddenly changes. The elements of nature that had kept them alive now threaten to destroy them. What will they do? There is little time to make a decision.

As you read this story, think about what you would do if the only way of life that you had ever known were suddenly in danger of being destroyed. Where would you go? What would you do?

VOCABULARY WORDS

rumbling (RUHM-blihng) low thundering sound
❖ Before the storm, we heard a *rumbling* coming from the east.

mosque (MAHSK) place of worship for Moslem people
❖ He went to the *mosque* several times a day to pray.

fetch (FEHCH) go get and bring back
❖ I am going to *fetch* more wood for the fire.

refugees (REHF-yoo-jees) people fleeing from danger
❖ During the war, many *refugees* fled to other countries.

spewing (SPYOO-ihng) pouring forth
❖ Water was *spewing* from the fountain.

taro (TAH-roh) tropical plant with a starchy root
❖ Some people eat *taro* root as often as we eat potatoes.

froth (FRAWTH) mass of small bubbles
❖ The ice cream soda had a thick layer of *froth*.

KEY WORDS

Krakatoa (krah-kah-TOH-uh) volcanic island in Indonesia, between the islands of Java and Sumatra
❖ We sailed to *Krakatoa* to see its volcano.

Sunda Strait (SOON-duh STRAYT) body of water running between Java and Sumatra, linking the Pacific and Indian oceans
❖ The ship reached the Pacific by passing through the *Sunda Strait*.

**W**hen Buyung turned his canoe toward home that afternoon in late August, he felt vaguely uneasy. That volcanic mountain on the nearby island of Krakatoa looked taller. He told himself that he must be going crazy or getting old. But another look at the towering mountain caused him to shudder.

Buyung had never set foot on Krakatoa. He and his family lived on the small island of Anjer, just a few miles to the west. Like many of the fishermen, he had heard about the superstitions about the evil spirits that lived under that big mountain on Krakatoa. So it wasn't unusual for Buyung to murmur a short prayer whenever he sailed past it in his canoe.

This time, however, he said the prayer twice. He couldn't shake the uneasy feeling that he got when he looked toward the mountain. When he finished the prayer for the second time, he thought that he heard a vague rumbling. Buyung shrugged. It wasn't unusual for the mountain to rumble now and then. This summer, though, it seemed to be doing it more than usual. On the other hand, maybe it was just his imagination.

As Buyung's canoe cut a clean, straight path through the Sunda Strait toward home, his mind eased. It had been a good day's fishing. He and his family would soon be eating well. Buyung lived with his wife, Dasima; his eldest son, Firman; Firman's wife; and Firman's two children. Tonight there would be enough fish for everyone at home.

Already the sun was dipping behind the mountains to the west. The brief tropical twilight would soon give way to darkness. After he secured his canoe, Buyung made his way to his village. Even after the long day on the water, there was a spring in his step as he neared his house. It is always a good feeling to be home, he thought, as he ducked under the broad, low overhang of the thatch roof.

Buyung found his wife, Dasima, working by the light of a kerosene lantern. She was slicing fruit for their dinner. Buyung set his heavy basket down and gestured to it with a smile.

"There you are!" He proudly drew six fish from the basket and set them in a silver row on the table. Dasima's eyes danced.

"Firman's favorite fish!"

The mention of their eldest son reminded Buyung that he needed Firman's help to mend some sails. From the time that he had been a very little boy, Firman had fished with his father. No one knew a canoe and its sails better. Now that Firman was married, however, he had gone to work in the rice fields with his father-in-law. Buyung had been left to fish alone.

Buyung sat down and watched his wife prepare the fish. For some reason, he was thinking about the mountain again. "Did you hear the mountain rumble today?" he asked her.

His wife looked up from her work. "We could hear it several times here on land. But it's been grumbling all May. All summer, it's fired cannon shots and coughed smoke." She tried to make it sound as if this meant nothing in particular.

"Who can know what will happen?" asked Buyung, a little uneasily. "Even the wise men at the mosque and Pastor Kamerbeeck at the Dutch mission school cannot tell us."

He paused and then asked: "Dasima, would you call me crazy if I told you that I thought the mountain was growing taller?" Dasima had stepped outside to fetch more fruit, and didn't hear him.

In fact, Krakatoa *was* growing taller—by nearly five hundred feet—because of the enormous pressure building up inside. Other people in the village had seen it. They were frightened as well, but they didn't know what to do about it. All of them tried to tell themselves that the mountain wasn't really acting any differently. Maybe the rumblings were increasing. That didn't necessarily mean that the volcano would erupt.

The next day, Buyung offered to work with his son in the rice paddies. In exchange, he expected Firman's help mending the sails.

They worked all morning in the fields. Then the heat of the midday sun, blazing down from directly overhead, became unbearable. Buyung and Firman sat in the shade of a grove of banana trees on the edge of the paddies. They began eating the sticky rice and strips of spicy buffalo meat that Dasima had made for them.

Suddenly, they heard a loud roar. Jumping up, they ran over to join their friend Teguh and some of the other farmers.

"Look!" Teguh cried. "The mountain!"

A broad column of smoke was pouring up from the top of Krakatoa, staining the sky. Flames crackled through the ink-black ash. Another explosion struck the men's ears.

Buyung grabbed his son's arm.

"The boat, Firman! We must help those people off the island!"

They ran quickly to the beach and readied the canoe. There was a good north breeze blowing, enough wind to bring them to Krakatoa by mid-afternoon.

A couple of hours later, they had neared the island. The explosions were more frequent now. The villagers of Krakatoa lined the beach. Canoes were everywhere. Firman had to be careful to avoid a collision.

111

All the rest of that afternoon, Buyung and his son helped to ferry the stranded villagers off Krakatoa. Several large fishing vessels in the straits took the refugees aboard. As the sun lowered in the west, Buyung and Firman could do no more. They turned their boat home.

When they beached their canoe an hour after sunset, Buying and Firman had to struggle through the crowd that had gathered on the shoreline to get to the village. The people of Anjer were close to panic. They wondered what the eruption would do to the seawater. Would it kill the fish?

Some villagers feared that the heavy ash spewing from the volcano would make a huge hole in the ocean floor. Water rushing to fill that hole could create waves

112

high enough to flood Anjer. At least, that's what the ancients had said. Stories about this happening had been passed down through the generations. No one was certain that they were true.

When Buyung and Firman got home, Dasima was frantic with worry.

"We must leave the village, my husband," she said. "We must go to higher ground before the great wave comes."

"Is anyone else leaving?" asked Buyung.

His wife shook her head. "Not yet," said his wife. "Most still wait to see what will happen. But I have become too frightened."

Buyung thought about those gigantic tidal waves that he had heard described in stories told by his grandfather. The waves were called *tsunami*. They traveled at superhuman speed and could destroy everything in their path. Supposedly, they could come after a volcanic eruption. Were the stories true?

Buyung was silent for a moment. "You are right, Dasima," he answered softly. "I do not know where we will go, but we will go higher. Get the children ready. We will leave as soon as we can."

Dasima disappeared with Firman's wife into the rear of the hut to prepare the young children. Within moments, they were ready to leave. They did not pack. This was a journey that no one had planned, traveling toward a destination that no one knew.

All night they walked, climbing ever upward. They passed the Dutch mission school and the rice fields and the taro plantations. Firman's eleven-year-old son had no trouble keeping up. Sometimes, though, Firman had to carry his younger son, Dirung, who was only four. They stopped briefly once at a village, where some farmers gave them black tea to drink.

An hour before sunrise, they had reached the upland plateau, and Buyung called a halt. They sat wearily in the shelter of some large banana trees at the edge of a forest. In between the mountain's ferocious blasts, they could hear the startled cries of the animals. That night, all the creatures of the forest seemed to be panicking.

The family fell asleep, worn out by their all-night journey. By morning, a deafening roar awakened them. Everyone sat bolt upright.

"Oh, no!" cried Dasima in horror, as they looked westward. Half of Krakatoa had been fired aloft into the sky. Lightning flashed, and the sea was a boiling froth. Time stood still as they watched earth, air, fire, and water mixing together in ways that no one had ever seen before.

Then they noticed something even stranger. Far out from shore, a huge wave suddenly curved above the surface of the sea. Firman was the first to spot it. Gripping Buyung's shoulder, he cried, "Tsunami, Father!"

Buyung's eyes locked on the huge wall of black water. It was as if it had come surging out of his grand-father's tales. Buyung struggled to think clearly. He glanced at the stout stems of the banana trees. Some of them grew two feet across and thirty feet high. Maybe they would save his family.

"Listen!" he cried. "If the wave reaches us, put your arms around the tree trunks and hold on as tight as you can. Firman, you hold a trunk with your wife and eldest son. Your mother and I will hold one with the little one." So the six of them held on to the tree trunks with all their might.

The black wall of water kept rushing toward them. They saw it reach the shore and lift docked canoes as if they were no more than dried leaves. Then it crashed

114

through the village below, leveling the huts and snapping the fruit trees.

Still the tsunami barreled forward, climbing the hill toward Buyung and his family. Now it swept over them while they strained to hold on to the banana trees.

Moments later, the great wave had passed them. They let go of their trees and rolled over in exhaustion. Finally, Firman's eldest son struggled to his feet and peered over the slope of the hill.

"Father!" he cried. "The town is gone!"

The others dragged themselves toward the slope. Below them, everything had been washed away. The homes, wagons, animals, and boats were all gone. The ground and what trees remained were coated with black ash.

Eventually, a rescue boat picked up Buyung and his family and took them to a neighboring island. For two and a half days, the sky was pitch-black above them from all the ash floating in the air. When it finally cleared, they learned that more than 30,000 people on and around Krakatoa had been killed. Of all the people who lived in their town, they were the only family that had survived.

READING FOR UNDERSTANDING

1. At the beginning of the story, what bothered Buyung about the appearance of the volcano on Krakatoa?

2. What was causing the volcano to look different than usual?

3. What happened to the volcano the next day, as Buyung and his son were working in the fields?

4. When Buyung's wife said that the volcano had been "grumbling all May," why did she try to make it sound as if it meant nothing in particular?

5. Why were the people of Anjer so panicked about the possibility of the fish being killed by the volcano?

6. When the volcano first erupted, no one but Buyung and his family decided to leave. Why do you think Buyung and Dasima made this decision?

RESPONDING TO THE STORY

Have you ever noticed that something seemed "not quite right," only to push it out of your mind? What happened afterward? Write a paragraph describing your experience.

REVIEWING VOCABULARY

Match each word on the left with the correct definition on the right.

1. taro
2. spewing
3. froth
4. rumbling
5. mosque
6. fetch
7. refugees

a. low thundering sound
b. mass of small bubbles
c. go get and bring back
d. place of worship for Moslem people
e. tropical plant with starchy root
f. people fleeing from danger
g. pouring forth

THINKING CRITICALLY ABOUT CULTURE

1. In this story, the people of the island are dependent upon the forces of nature. They have few machines or modern conveniences. How does this compare with life in this country? What are the advantages and disadvantages of each way of life?

2. Buyung and his family relied on stories passed down through generations. These stories entertain and provide information. How accurate are these stories? How did they help Buyung and his family deal with life in their village?

3. Suppose Buyung and his family had come to the United States after the eruption looking for a new home. How do you think they would have fared here?

CRISIS AT CALLESPAN LIGHTHOUSE

Rafaela Ellis

Imagine yourself as a lighthouse keeper on the lonely, rocky Maine coast. A stormy night is brewing out at sea. You spot a ship that's in trouble. The winds are howling. The waves are crashing. It would be dangerous to go out-side. But there are people who need you—and you know your duty.

In the story that you are about to read, a father and his daughter risk their lives to do their duty. They have no choice. They are lighthouse keepers.

Lighthouses are less important now than they once were. The reason is that most modern ships have advanced electronic equipment to help them avoid rocks and reefs. But equipment cannot always protect a ship when the sea is in a wild fury. Lighthouse keepers can still save lives—as this story shows.

VOCABULARY WORDS

pelted (PEHLT-uhd) struck, pounded on
❖ During the heavy storm, the rain *pelted* the roof.

dread (DREHD) fear very much
❖ Luis and I *dread* the weekly math quiz at school.

endearment (ehn-DIHR-muhnt) affection
❖ She used many terms of *endearment* when speaking with the children.

momentarily (moh-muhn-TEHR-uh-lee) briefly, lasting for only a moment
❖ After the screen flickered *momentarily*, it went dead.

superstitious (soo-per-STIH-shuhs) having beliefs based on fear
❖ Avoiding action on Friday the 13th is *superstitious*.

blustery (BLUS-tuhr-ee) stormy
❖ It was a *blustery* March morning, so he put on a heavy coat.

anxiety (ang-ZY-uh-tee) uneasiness over a possible future event
❖ He experienced *anxiety* each time that the airplane bounced.

summit (SUM-iht) highest point
❖ They struggled all morning to reach the mountain's *summit*.

trio (TREE-oh) group of three
❖ A *trio* of gulls perched on the dock, looking for scraps.

 **S**tefan Holmstrom stood at the top of the Callespan Lighthouse and looked out over the choppy Atlantic Ocean. The setting sun was casting a lovely golden glow across the tops of the waves, but Captain Holmstrom was too worried to notice. A storm was brewing out at sea. For a lighthouse keeper like Captain Holmstrom, a storm means trouble.

"These late fall gales come up quickly," he thought. "I hope that ship on the horizon is keeping in touch with someone on shore." He checked the lighthouse's switches and polished its enormous lenses. Captain Holmstrom had spent 30 years at sea in the merchant marines, in command of a cargo ship that carried silk and china to the United States from the Far East. He had sailed all the world's oceans. He knew how fierce the Atlantic Ocean off Maine's coast could be when fall winds began to blow.

As the sun set in the western sky, Holmstrom saw the first streaks of lightning flash. The BOOM of thunder that quickly followed told him that a storm was approaching. Rain began to fall. Large drops pelted the lighthouse window. Captain Holmstrom reached for the control switch. The time had come to set the light's warning signal. The pattern of the light's flashes would alert passing ships to the danger that lurked off Callespan's rocky shore.

"Pop," a voice called from the bottom of the lighthouse's stairs. "Do you need some help up there?"

"Come on up, Inga," Captain Holmstrom responded. "I can always use an extra pair of eyes on a stormy night like this."

Inga Holmstrom slowly climbed up the narrow, winding staircase that led to the top of the lighthouse.

120

In the six years that her father had been operating the Callespan Lighthouse, Inga had come to dread nights like this. She knew that her father would not leave his lighthouse perch until the storm had passed or morning had come. She couldn't let him stay up there all alone, could she? She knew that he was an able lighthouse keeper and a strong man. But, he was also her father, and she worried about him.

"I've brought you a thermos of coffee, Pop," Inga said when she reached the top of the stairs.

"Thank you, little one," he said, taking the thermos. Although his daughter was almost eighteen years old, Stefan Holmstrom still thought of her as his little one. Inga had grown to love her father's term of endearment, spoken in his thick Swedish accent.

"So, do you think there will be trouble tonight?" Inga asked.

Stefan Holmstrom put down his binoculars and looked at his daughter. "On a night like tonight, Inga, we can only hope that no trouble comes."

Suddenly, a bright flash of lightning lit up the sea and sky. Inga and her father stared out at the churning ocean, lit up momentarily by the burst of light.

"There's a boat out there," Inga said.

"Yes, little one, I've been watching it. I thought it was moving away from us, but it seems to be getting closer."

"Don't they understand the light's signal?" Inga asked. "They're coming so close. They could hit one of the rocky reefs off shore!"

"Now, now," said Captain Holmstrom. "Don't panic, Inga. Remember, we've been here for six years, and we haven't had a disaster yet."

As soon as the words were spoken, Stefan Holmstrom regretted saying them. His years at sea had made him superstitious. Now, as he brought his binoculars to his eyes, he felt a knot in the pit of his stomach. The boat that he had been tracking was being capsized by the crashing surf.

"Pop," cried Inga. "They're going down!"

"All right, Inga. Follow me!" Holmstrom ordered. Like a sailor on one of her father's ships, Inga responded instantly. The pair flew down the lighthouse steps, grabbing their life vests off hooks next to the door, as they ran out into the blustery night.

Through the torrential rain, Stefan Holmstrom and his daughter ran to the edge of the shoreline. As they reached the land's end, they could see that the boat had hit a reef. Then they saw a shadowy figure staggering up the rocky beach.

"Help! Help us!" shouted a man, as Inga and her father ran toward him. "The rest of my family is still on that boat!"

Without saying a word, Stefan Holmstrom pulled off his boots, slipped on his life vest, and plunged into the chilly water. He swam toward the sinking vessel, fighting all the way against the strong current and the wind-swept waves. When he reached the reef, Holmstrom saw the dim outlines of several passengers clinging to the damaged boat. He reached out and grabbed the person closest to him. It was a young boy about ten years old.

"Hang on, son," Holmstrom cried. With the boy clinging to his back, the captain swam toward shore.

"Pop!" Inga cried, as her father stumbled across the rocks with the little boy in his arms. "Thank heavens you're all right!"

"I am, little one," her father responded.

"There are two more people out there, Pop. This man, Mr. Matthews, says it was their first time out in a brand-new boat. They didn't know how to handle it. They lost their sense of direction and didn't understand the light's signal."

"I've got to go back for them," Stefan Holmstrom said. Before Inga could argue, her father dove back into the black ocean. Again he returned with a frightened, grateful survivor in his arms—Mrs. Matthews. She stood on the beach shaking uncontrollably as her husband ran to put his arms around her.

Finally, fatigue and the cold overtook Stefan Holmstrom. He collapsed, exhausted, at his daughter's feet. He didn't think that he could make one more trip.

Inga bent down to cradle her father's head.

"I . . . I did . . . all I could . . .," the lighthouse keeper gasped.

"Oh, Pop," said Inga, "you did so much."

Inga took off her jacket and wrapped it around her shivering father. As she pushed her father's hair out of his eyes, Inga heard someone crying. She looked up and saw Mrs. Matthews standing before her.

"My mother is still on the boat," the woman sobbed.

Immediately, Stefan Holmstrom began to rise, but Inga pushed him down. "Oh no you don't, Pop," said Inga. "You're too exhausted. You can't make it."

Mrs. Matthews looked at Inga and saw the anxiety on her face. "Sir," she said, turning to Captain Holmstrom, "you've done enough. I can't let you risk your life again."

"But your mother—" said Holmstrom.

"She can't still be alive, can she?" asked the woman. Tears were streaming down her face. "It's been too long. She's seventy-seven years old. She's very strong, but I don't think that she could survive this long."

"There may still be a chance," Holmstrom said.

"But you can't go," Inga said to her father. "You're too tired." Inga looked at Mrs. Matthews. "I'm sorry for your mother, really I am. But my father has done enough."

"It's all right," said the woman, wiping her eyes. "I don't think that she could have made it anyway. I appreciate everything that you've done." Then she dissolved into tears.

Stefan Holmstrom knew what he had to do. He was the keeper of the light. He was a man of the sea. He remembered his words back at the top of the lighthouse: "We haven't had a disaster yet." Maybe there was still a chance to avoid a disaster now.

Holmstrom stood up and walked calmly toward the water as Inga ran after him. "Don't do it, Pop, I'll go," she cried.

124

"No," said Holmstrom sternly. "I'm going."

Stefan Holmstrom threw off Inga's jacket and dove again into the crashing sea. He swam forward, his muscles burning, as he labored, stroke after stroke. His legs felt numb. Still, he pushed on. Finally, he reached the boat. Only a small tip of planking remained above the water's surface. No one was clinging to it.

The captain was about to turn back when he heard a strange sound coming from farther out in the water. Looking out, he saw Mrs. Matthews' mother struggling to keep hold of a rock sticking up in the sea.

"Hang on!" Holmstrom cried, as he swam toward the frightened woman.

"Oh, thank goodness!" the woman said, as Holmstrom reached out for her. "I don't know how much longer I could have lasted."

"Now hold on tight," Holmstrom said. The woman grabbed onto his belt, and Holmstrom began to swim forward. The weight of his passenger, combined with his fatigue, made the journey slow going. Holmstrom struggled, as wave after wave crashed into him, pushing him back toward the open ocean. Suddenly, he felt the old woman lose her grip and start to go under. He reached behind him and pulled her above the surface.

"I can't hold on," she sputtered.

"Then I'll hold on to you," Holmstrom said. He put one arm under the woman's back and used the other to begin swimming again toward the lighthouse, his lighthouse. He wondered if he would ever again stand at its summit. With each stroke, he doubted it more. His strength was leaving him. Finally, he could swim no more. Stefan Holmstrom felt himself going under.

Inga Holmstrom watched as her father sank into the dark ocean, about twenty yards from shore. Now, it was she who sprang into action. Without wasting a moment, Inga threw on her life vest, plunged into the water, and swam toward the drowning pair.

Inga's arms cut through the churning water in quick, sharp strokes. She remembered the words that her father had taught her to recite when he was teaching her how to swim: "Stroke, stroke, breath. Stroke, stroke, breath." The rhythm of the phrase kept her moving.

Within minutes, she reached the spot where she had seen her father's orange life vest. Looking around, Inga saw her father going under. Inga swam over and grabbed his arm, pulling hard. Her father popped up, gasping, above the water's surface, followed by the exhausted woman.

"Just a few more feet," Inga cried, as she swam with them toward shore. Her father helped her pull the older woman through the water. As she neared the land's edge, those on the beach splashed into the sea and helped drag the trio to safety.

"Inga," her father panted, as he tumbled to the sand. "The water was so rough. How did you do it?"

Inga Holmstrom smiled through her tears. "Like father, like daughter," she answered.

Stefan Holmstrom lay on the rocky ground, looking up. Above him, he could see the strong beam of Callespan Lighthouse shining across the sky. As he watched the beacon blink against the blackness, he said a silent prayer of thanks for his daughter, his lighthouse, and his lifelong friendship with the sea.

READING FOR UNDERSTANDING

1. Arrange the following incidents in the order in which they occurred:
   (a) Stefan saw Mrs. Matthews' mother clinging to a rock.
   (b) Inga brought Stefan a thermos of coffee.
   (c) Inga plunged into the ocean.
   (d) Stefan rescued the little boy.
   (e) Stefan saw the first lightning flashes.
2. Where did the story take place?
3. What did the man on the beach tell Stefan? What action did Stefan take without saying a word?
4. Why did Stefan try to rescue Mrs. Matthews' mother, even though he was exhausted?
5. After everyone was safe, how did Inga explain her brave action to her father?

RESPONDING TO THE STORY

Pick out one scene in the story that made an impression on you. What about that scene made it meaningful? Explain your reaction in a paragraph, using details from the scene.

REVIEWING VOCABULARY

Match each word on the left with the correct definition on the right.

1. momentarily   a. uneasiness
2. dread   b. affection
3. summit   c. having beliefs based on fear
4. anxiety   d. group of three
5. blustery   e. fear very much
6. trio   f. stormy
7. endearment   g. briefly
8. superstitious   h. highest point
9. pelted   i. struck, pounded on

THINKING CRITICALLY

1. What do you think life in a lighthouse would be like? Would it be lonely? What would you do every day to keep yourself alert?
2. What did the story suggest about the importance of safety training for boaters? Do you think that people who go out in boats have an obligation to follow safety rules? Why?
3. What do you think made Stefan and Inga risk their lives for others? Are there times when you think that you would risk your own life to save someone else? Explain.
4. Stefan barely escaped with his life. At the end of the story, why do you think he was thankful for his "lifelong friendship with the sea"?

Unit 4
FREEZING FEARS

ONE WARM COAT
Brenda Lane Richardson

Imagine yourself on a hiking trail when a snowstorm suddenly develops. What if you have no warm clothing and no shelter for the night? Suppose that you become injured. Would you be able to survive a night in the great outdoors under such difficult conditions?

Perhaps you feel that you are well prepared for this kind of situation. But you'll still want to match your survival skills against those of the two girls in "One Warm Coat."

Tammy and Lee's hike in the Blue Ridge Mountains starts out as a nature walk. Tammy thinks that she knows the woods really well. Yet, it is her cousin Lee's common sense that gets the girls out of a dangerous situation. Read the story to see just how dangerous it is.

VOCABULARY WORDS

taunting (TAWNT-ihng) making fun of, mocking
❖ The mouse seemed to be *taunting* the cat.

considerably (kuhn-SIHD-uhr-uh-blee) substantially, a lot
❖ Although it was cold in the morning, the weather had warmed up *considerably* by noon.

vapor (VAY-puhr) visible moisture, such as fog or steam
❖ On very cold days, you can see your breath in short bursts of white *vapor*.

sneered (SNEERD) showed scorn or contempt
❖ Lee *sneered* at Tammy's hiking boots.

sulky (SUL-kee) disagreeable, resentful
❖ From his *sulky* expression, we could tell that he was not satisfied with our apology.

hysterical (hihs-TAIR-uh-kuhl) uncontrollably excited or wild
❖ When the fire broke out in the theater, most of the audience panicked and became *hysterical*.

frostbite (FRAWHST-byt) damage to body tissues caused by exposure to intense cold
❖ Mountain climbers must be careful to avoid *frostbite*.

KEY WORD

Blue Ridge Mountains eastern range of the Appalachian Mountains, extending south from southern Pennsylvania to northern Georgia
❖ The girls went on a beetle-collecting expedition in the *Blue Ridge Mountains*.

**Tammy and her cousin Lee** were hiking in the Blue Ridge Mountains. The two fourteen year olds were hoping to add to Tammy's beetle collection. Lee was tagging along only because her cousin had bet a cheeseburger that she wasn't tough enough to keep up with her. As far as Lee was concerned, she'd already won. The day was almost over, and Lee was not only keeping up with her cousin but was also enjoying herself. She wouldn't admit that to Tammy, though.

Suddenly, Tammy tripped over a huge log and lay sprawled across the trail. Lee helped her up and dusted her off while saying, "Try taking your nose out of that bug book, and maybe you'll find some bugs!"

Growing up next door to one another, in a Virginia suburb, made the two girls more like sisters than cousins. Tammy was only a few weeks older, but Lee called her "Tammy the Teacher" because Lee felt that her cousin was always trying to teach her things. Today's "lesson" was supposed to be about the wonders of nature. Tammy had insisted that if Lee spent just one day away from the telephone and her CD player, she would discover a whole new world in the woods. Tammy was right. The woods in early winter were unbelievably beautiful. But Lee couldn't admit that. Tammy was wrong. She promised herself to stick to the story that Tammy was wrong.

The wind carried a few large snowflakes toward them. Lee hugged herself for warmth and then immediately regretted that she had. Tammy observed her and responded: "I told you to wear that heavy jacket. It can get cold out here. You should have listened to me."

"Yeah, yeah, yeah, you always know everything," said Lee. "That coat was so out of style that our great-

great grandmother would have refused to wear it. Besides, I'm not at all cold." To make her point, she quickly pulled off her woolen cap and her gloves, while singing loudly to drown out Tammy's words. The snow was falling heavily now. They hiked another half-mile before Lee thought of asking: "You do know where you're going, don't you?"

It was difficult to determine where they were going, with the snow falling down around them and blanketing the ground. Maybe they were only traveling in circles. Lee anxiously waited to hear Tammy's familiar voice saying that of course she knew where they were. She simply wanted to hear her say that they finally were going home. When her cousin didn't answer, Lee spun around, but Tammy wasn't there!

Lee doubled back, looking all around her for Tammy and calling out her name loudly. With a sigh of relief, she heard her cousin taunting her. "What's wrong? Don't tell me that you missed me!" mocked Tammy, appearing out of the snow.

Lee took a deep breath. She was badly frightened and moved in closer to Tammy, who was busy reading a trail map and checking a compass. Since her cousin wasn't watching her, Lee slowly slipped her gloves back on. The snow seemed to make everything feel a lot colder. In a half hour, it appeared that at least an inch of snow had fallen.

Lee repeated her question, but this time with less confidence in her voice. "You know where you're going, don't you?" Tammy responded by muttering something that Lee couldn't understand. The wind had picked up considerably and seemed to be carrying away her cousin's voice. And what was that strange expression on Tammy's face? Lee couldn't remember seeing it there before. Could this possibly mean that Tammy, of all

133

people, was embarrassed? That meant that they were lost in the woods for sure. Now, Lee was really getting frightened. She knew that she was breathing harder because the air came from her mouth in short bursts of white vapor. "What are we going to do?" she asked, feeling desperate.

Tammy responded in her usual know-it-all tone: "I noticed that we passed a hut not too long ago. I guess that we'd better go back to it. Somebody is sure to come looking for us. That way we'll be safe while we wait."

"Oh, brother!" Lee said to herself. Of all the times for her oh-so-perfect cousin to make a mistake! Why did it have to be here in the Blue Ridge Mountains, with the snow swirling about them and the wind picking up? Lee was far too angry to be cold. Fed up, she pulled her stocking cap off and stomped on it. Tammy quickly picked it up and held it out to her.

"Put this back on and keep those gloves on, too! Don't you know that you lose most of your body heat through your head and hands and feet? Those are the most important parts of your body to keep warm." Tammy stared down at her cousin's sneakers. She'd tried convincing Lee to wear heavy hiking boots, but Lee simply had sneered at them.

Lee pulled her hat on, but her face kept its sulky expression. Tammy lost what little patience she had left. "Now, look here, I'm not going to baby-sit you. You're a big girl. I told you that I'll get us to that cabin, and I will. One night in a cabin certainly isn't going to kill you."

"One night!" yelled Lee. "Do you really think that it will only take them until tomorrow to find us?"

Tammy no longer heard her clearly. She already was moving back along the path from which they'd come.

134

Lee hurried to keep up with her, trying to convince herself that Tammy was right. One night wasn't so bad, and she'd really have something to tell her friends about when they finally got out of this mess.

Luckily, the door to the hut was unlocked. Lee wasn't impressed. "No wonder it's unlocked," she said to herself, as she looked around her at the dark space, which was only about the size of a closet. "Who on earth would want to get in here?" But she was determined not to complain out loud about anything else. She didn't want Tammy telling everybody that she'd acted like a big baby when they finally got back home. She had to admit, though, that she was beginning to feel like a baby. For one thing, she was cold; in fact, she was practically freezing. And what would they eat besides those disgusting tuna fish sandwiches?

Tammy began gathering up pine needles, explaining to Lee that they'd help keep them warm when they slept on the floor. Still furious with her cousin, Lee started putting her pile of pine needles as far from Tammy's pile as possible. She simply didn't want to be anywhere near her.

Tammy's voice interrupted Lee's angry thoughts. "You may not want to be anywhere near me, but the only way that we'll really keep warm is by sharing our body heat."

By now, the hut was in total darkness. Lee felt strange talking to somebody whom she couldn't even see. "I'm just tired of hearing about how much you know," she murmured into the darkness. "If you know so much, why on earth are we lost?"

Lee expected another lecture from her cousin, but what she heard instead frightened her. Tammy's voice sounded just like a little girl's. "I'm scared, too, Lee. I'm really sorry that I got us into this mess."

135

Lee found herself giggling, and she reached out for Tammy's hand. "Did I actually hear you say that you were sorry about something? You know what? You were absolutely right about that coat. I'd give anything for one warm coat right now."

Somehow, the two girls made it through the night without freezing, although they didn't get much sleep. When Lee awoke early the next morning, stiff from the cold, hard floor, she ran to the window. She was amazed to see how high the snowdrifts were. It was still snowing. She shook Tammy awake.

This time, it took them almost three times as long to climb through the snow back to where they'd turned around the evening before. Tammy took her pocketknife out and marked the trees with arrows to remind herself of where they'd been. The arrows would also serve as signs to anyone who might be searching for them. Finally, Lee took over the tree marking. She was willing to do almost anything to keep her mind off the numbing cold.

Suddenly, Lee stubbed her toe on a rock hidden in the snow, stumbled and fell onto Tammy. Because Lee was holding the open knife, its tip grazed Tammy's leg. Tammy shrieked in pain. The blood sickened Lee, but she forced herself to examine the cut. The wound looked clean and not particularly deep, but it was bleeding heavily. Blood seemed to be everywhere in the snow, and Tammy became hysterical.

Lee surprised herself by remaining calm. Then she spoke softly to Tammy, saying that she was sorry for her mistake. She tore a piece of cloth from the sleeve of her own blouse and tied the wound. Tammy's sobs softened, but still she was unable to walk. What would they do now? The snow had stopped falling, but the wind whipped against their faces.

136

Lee began talking to herself to boost her confidence. Maybe she didn't have all the book knowledge that Tammy had, but she did have her common sense. She vaguely remembered something from her old first-aid class. Tammy needed warmth. Grabbing a thick piece of a fallen branch, she began digging a cave out of the snow, against the side of a large rock. In about half an hour, she had cleared away enough snow to provide a shelter for them both. Then she helped her cousin limp into the cave. At least, it sheltered them from the wind.

"What next?" she asked herself. Then Lee began gathering twigs and small pieces of wood and laying them at the base of the large rock, where the cave was. How lucky she felt that they had brought a couple of packs of matches. It took all but three of the matches to get a fire going. The fire kept them warm and cheered her cousin's mood.

Later that morning, adults from a search party found them and were surprised to discover the girls in such good condition. Neither had frostbite, and Tammy's wound was in surprisingly good shape.

Tammy gave Lee all the credit, but Lee remained quiet and didn't boast. Maybe she didn't know much about bugs or hiking. But one thing that she did know was how to take charge when the going got really rough. She knew that she had shown her true colors in a time of great stress. She discovered that some things are not learned from books, and that there are things— such as common sense—that aren't learned at all. You either have it, or you don't.

READING FOR UNDERSTANDING

1. Arrange the following incidents in the order in which they occurred:
   (a) The girls found the door to the hut unlocked.
   (b) Lee dug a makeshift cave in the snow.
   (c) Adults from a search party found the girls.
   (d) Tammy apologized to Lee and admitted that she was scared.
   (e) Lee's knife cut Tammy's leg.
2. Where did the story take place?
3. What were some of the reasons the two girls had trouble getting along on the hike?
4. What were some of the survival strategies that Tammy talked about or used in the story? What were some of the survival strategies that Lee used?
5. At what point in this story did Lee's attitude change? How did it change? How and when did Tammy's attitude change?
6. What did Lee learn about herself in this story? What is the story's message, or central meaning?

RESPONDING TO THE STORY

The two girls in this story had different strengths. Tammy had learned a lot from books, while her cousin Lee discovered that she had a lot of common sense. Which of the characters is more like you? Explain in a paragraph.

REVIEWING VOCABULARY

Match each word on the left with the correct definition on the right.

1. sneered
2. considerably
3. hysterical
4. vapor
5. taunting
6. frostbite
7. sulky

a. making fun of
b. substantially, a lot
c. showed scorn or contempt
d. disagreeable, resentful
e. visible moisture, such as fog or steam
f. uncontrollably excited or wild
g. damage to body tissues caused by intense cold

THINKING CRITICALLY

1. You learned from the story that Tammy and Lee were both fourteen years old and had grown up next door to each other. Each girl had strengths and weaknesses. What were some of Tammy's strengths? What were some of her weaknesses?

2. This story painted a vivid picture of each girl's personality. It also showed the changes that each went through. How exactly did each girl change? What details in the story showed these changes?

3. Lee may not have been as educated as Tammy. But at the end of the story, she learned to value her own knowledge. How did this story prove that knowledge doesn't always come from books?

DEFEATING THE WHITE DEATH

Rafaela Ellis

Have you ever tried downhill skiing? For millions of skiers, there's nothing quite like their favorite sport. Most of the time, danger couldn't be further from their minds.

Yet, an avalanche can mean sudden danger and death! A huge mass of snow tumbling out of control down a mountainside can cause panic for even the most experienced skiers. In order to survive, one has to overcome fear while thinking clearly.

Linda Rodriguez was an expert member of the ski patrol. In the following story, you'll see how Linda fought bravely against panic when she was overtaken by every skier's greatest fear: the White Death.

VOCABULARY WORDS

avalanche (AV-uh-lanch) mass of loosened snow that suddenly and swiftly slides down a mountain
❖ An *avalanche* means great danger for skiers.

subsided (sub-SYD-ihd) slowed down
❖ After the showers *subsided*, the game continued.

wound (WOWND) turned or twisted
❖ On a map, she saw how the trail *wound* through the woods.

dislodge (dihs-LAHDJ) move or force from a position
❖ Try as we might, we could not *dislodge* the heavy boulder from the road.

baton (buh-TAHN) slender stick used by a conductor in directing an orchestra
❖ When the conductor raised his *baton*, the audience knew that the concert was about to begin.

infirmary (ihn-FER-muh-ree) room or building that serves as a short-term hospital
❖ When Ferris began to have flu symptoms, he was admitted to the *infirmary*.

lobbed (LAHBD) slowly thrown or tossed in a high curve
❖ He *lobbed* the softball to the child in an easy, under-hand throw.

It **was early morning** during the busiest time of year at the Grand Mountain Ski Resort in the Rocky Mountains of Colorado. Hundreds of skiers would be skiing the mountains today. The weight and movement of skiers gliding down the mountain could cause loose snow to come crashing down.

A controlled avalanche was being started in order to avoid an unexpected life-threatening avalanche. Linda Rodriguez watched from outside the lodge, as the huge sheet of snow tumbled down the mountain, increasing in size and speed. In six years as a ski patrol leader, Linda had never gotten tired of watching a controlled avalanche. She loved the whole idea of it: using explosives to cause a snow slide in order to prevent one from occurring when skiers were on the slopes.

The snow of the controlled avalanche cascaded down Grand Mountain with a thunderous roar. Linda was filled with awe. As often as this technique had been used in the Rockies, she never got used to this display of nature's terrible power.

Skiers call an avalanche the White Death, because it was almost impossible to survive if you were caught in it. Avalanches had been known to topple fifty-foot pine trees and crush houses in their paths. What chance did a person have against such a force?

"Looks like our controlled avalanche has taken care of the loose stuff," Linda said to her team, as the roar subsided.

Karen Heil, her assistant, headed back inside the lodge. "I'm going to take a hot bath," she said, "before the crowd arrives."

"I'm going skiing," said Linda. "I want to enjoy these slopes before everybody else gets out here."

Half an hour later, Linda snapped on her skis and headed for Deadman's Run. It was the most difficult trail at Grand Mountain Resort.

She paused at the top of the run, looking at the trail as it wound below her. There were no tracks, no ruts left by previous skiers. It was fresh, and it was all hers.

She started down. Her skis cut into the white powder, leaving deep marks behind them. She was picking up speed now, heading toward the S-curve, the halfway point in the run. As she leaned into the curve, she heard a loud BANG. She recognized the sound—it was the boom that an explosive made when it was fired into the mountain. The controlled avalanche, she remembered, had been finished half an hour ago. Linda stopped in her tracks and turned to search for the source of the blast.

Looking up the mountain, Linda froze in terror. Something was terribly wrong. An unexploded shell from this morning's work must have exploded. Now she could see that a mass of snow was barreling straight down toward her.

Linda Rodriguez was about to be caught in the White Death.

Linda's mind went into full gear, remembering the rules that she had taught her patrol team a thousand times. "You can't outrun an avalanche," she heard herself saying. "If you're ever caught in one, try to 'swim' on top of it, just like body surfing on the surface of the ocean." The sound of the approaching snow slide was deafening. She would have to put her training into practice right away. There was no time to take off her skis; they would fall off as soon as the avalanche reached her.

Suddenly, Linda was overtaken. She felt herself tumbling with the falling snow. She tried to swim on the surface by moving her arms in a free-style stroke. She strained to keep her eyes open, but all that she could see was a whirl of light and darkness.

Linda closed her eyes as she continued to tumble down the mountain. Farther and farther she fell, struggling to stay on the surface of the snowy wave that carried her. Then, as suddenly as it had begun, her tumbling stopped. "It's over," Linda thought. "I must be at the bottom." When she tried to open her eyes, though, she couldn't seem to pry her lids apart. Then she realized what had happened. Although her eyes were open, there was nothing to see.

She was not on the surface. Linda was buried under the avalanche.

"Don't panic," she told herself. "Just don't." She reminded herself that the first step to surviving any dangerous situation was to stay calm. That was going to be hard, though, given what she knew. She had only about thirty minutes to find a way out of the black pit in which she was trapped. After that, most people buried in an avalanche run out of oxygen or freeze to death. Linda had to move quickly.

Her first step was to find out whether she was upside down or right-side up. Luckily, there seemed to be a pocket of air around her face. She decided to use a trick she'd learned in patrol training. You spit. If your face gets wet, you're right-side up. If the spit goes away from your face, you're upside down. She may have been buried under snow, but the laws of gravity still applied. Linda spit and felt a wet splash on her chin. She was right-side up. Now she knew in which direction to move.

Moving wasn't easy. Although there was a pocket of air around her face, the rest of her body was packed in hard snow. She tried to move her legs. They wouldn't budge. The only thing she could move was her right arm. Maybe she could get it to move a little more.

"The hardest thing," Linda remembered telling her patrol team, "is to overcome your fear, to think clearly." Now, she struggled against her own fear to remain calm. The worst part was the noise. With every small movement, she could hear the crackling and hissing of the snow mass moving around her. The sounds filled her with terror.

"Steady," Linda thought to herself. "Just try to move that arm."

Linda kept pushing upward with her right arm. How long had she been buried? She knew every minute counted. But she was making ever-so-slight progress with each effort of the arm. She used her fingers to dig into the snow, scooping tiny amounts into the hole created by the movement of her arm.

Then, as Linda's gloved fingers continued to dig, they came upon something hard. Linda knew that rocks and debris often fell with the snow during an avalanche. This object felt long and thin. Maybe it was a tree branch. Eventually, Linda was able to get her thumb and forefinger around the unknown object.

Linda began shaking whatever it was she held. It felt like a stick. Maybe she could dislodge some snow with the movement. Then slowly but surely she would use it to tunnel herself out. The snow packed around her was hard, but she could feel—and hear—it cracking as she pushed the object back and forth. After a few moments, she got her entire hand around the stick. Now she could shake it more vigorously.

For the first time since the ordeal began, Linda felt she was making progress. She kept shaking the stick and got into a kind of rhythm. She recalled a chant that the ski patrol used when digging out an injured skier: "Snow is cold, and snow is white. Skiers know that snow's all right." It kept them focused, kept them moving together. Now, she recited it to herself as she moved the stick back and forth.

The noises were getting louder now. The cracking and hissing of the moving snow was terrifying. The echo of her own breathing added to that terror. Linda continued chanting, trying to drown out the frightening noises.

Suddenly, she heard a loud "swoosh." It was like the sound of an enormous can being opened. Then, for the first time since she had stopped tumbling down the mountain, Linda Rodriguez saw something. A small stream of light pierced the darkness.

"I think we've got her!" she heard a voice yell. "Over here!" Then Linda heard other voices and the sound of shovels hitting the snow above her.

"I see her arm!" someone yelled. "Linda! Linda, can you hear me?"

Linda tried to speak, but nothing came out. Still, she heard the digging continue. In a matter of seconds, someone was brushing the snow off her face. Linda looked up and saw Karen and the other members of the ski patrol standing at the rim of the four-foot hole in which she lay.

"Are you all right?" asked Karen.

"I . . . I think so," Linda said.

Carefully, the patrol members lifted Linda out of the hole and placed her on a stretcher.

"I don't think anything's broken," Linda said, after carefully moving her left arm and her legs.

"You were lucky," said Karen. "When we heard that blast, we thought you were a goner. We knew that you were up here skiing. Thank goodness for that ski pole."

"Ski pole?" said Linda with confusion.

"Your ski pole was sticking out of the snow," said Karen. "At first we thought that maybe you lost it when you fell. But then it started moving. It was rocking back and forth like a conductor's baton! That's how we knew you were under there—and still alive!"

"That's right," said Linda, with a surprised laugh. "I am still alive, aren't I?"

From her bed in the Grand Mountain infirmary, Linda saw the mountain looming before her. A heavy snow had fallen overnight. Linda watched as the ski patrol set to work on the side of the mountain. They were aiming explosives at a mass of snow on the mountain's eastern face, where Deadman's Run was covered in white. Linda heard the familiar BANG as the shell was lobbed into the mountain.

She watched as the controlled avalanche came cascading down. Every skier's greatest fear: the White Death. Now she had seen it face to face—and gotten out alive!

READING FOR UNDERSTANDING

1. Arrange the following incidents in the order in which they occurred:
   (a) Karen told Linda that Linda's ski pole was sticking out of the snow.
   (b) Linda used a trick to find out if she was right-side up.
   (c) At the halfway point in the run, Linda heard a loud noise.
   (d) Linda told her team that she was going skiing.
   (e) Carefully, the patrol members placed Linda on a stretcher.
2. Why do you think that Linda chose the most difficult trail?
3. About how much time do skiers have to dig themselves out if they are buried in an avalanche? Give two reasons why that time is so limited.
4. What was the object that Linda found with her fingers? How did this object save her?
5. What are some of the ways in which Linda's knowledge and skiing experience helped her to survive?

RESPONDING TO THE STORY

This story tells of a woman who refused to panic when she was caught in a life-or-death situation. What are some of the ways that you overcome fear? Write about them in a paragraph.

REVIEWING VOCABULARY

Match each word on the left with the correct definition on the right.

1. baton   **a.** force from a position
2. lobbed   **b.** moving mass of loosened snow
3. infirmary
4. dislodge   **c.** turned or twisted
5. avalanche   **d.** slowed down
6. subsided   **e.** conductor's stick
7. wound   **f.** short-term hospital
     g. thrown or tossed slowly

THINKING CRITICALLY

1. What character strengths and mental skills did Linda's training for ski patrol give her?

2. After she was caught in the avalanche, Linda recalled telling her ski patrol team: "The hardest thing is to overcome your fear, to think clearly." Think about your own experiences with fear. Why do you feel that this statement is true?

3. What does this story suggest to you about the power of nature? How does it make you feel about the relationship of human beings to nature?

THE DRUM OF THE LAW

Joyce Haines

For over half a century, Chinese workers played a major role in construction projects in the United States. The Transcontinental Railroad, finished in 1869, is one such project. Another is the Golden Gate Bridge in San Francisco, California, which opened in 1937.

Laboring under difficult conditions, the Chinese often performed highly dangerous jobs with great skill. Yet, Chinese workers faced cruel discrimination because of their language and customs. Like the Huang brothers in "The Drum of the Law," Chinese workers often risked their lives to do their jobs. For them, it was a matter of honor— and survival.

VOCABULARY WORDS

dynamite (DY-nuh-myt) a powerful explosive
❖ The miners used *dynamite* to blast through the rock.

harass (huh-RAS) attack or bother
❖ My mother said that she would *harass* me until I started my term paper.

heathens (HEE-thuhnz) persons who do not believe in the God of the Bible
❖ Because the workers did not share his faith, the boss called them *heathens*.

plagued (PLAYGD) badly troubled
❖ That low-lying area near the river is *plagued* every year by flooding.

trudged (TRUJD) walked wearily
❖ The tired miners *trudged* home at the end of each shift.

sheer (SHIR) extremely steep
❖ The Grand Canyon has many *sheer* slopes.

shock (SHAHK) the slowing down of the body's circulatory system
❖ After the car accident, the woman went into *shock*.

KEY WORDS

Beijing (bay-JIHNG) capital city of China
❖ Before they went to see the Great Wall of China, they stayed for three days in *Beijing*.

Sierras (see-ER-uhz) the Sierra Nevada (Spanish for "snowy range") mountain range in eastern California
❖ Building the railroad in the high *Sierras* was a difficult task.

**The Huang brothers** knew how to survive. Nothing stopped Liu, Tsun, and Chih. No desert, no river, no mountain was an obstacle. Since leaving their home in Beijing, the Huangs had built cedar snowsheds and laid railroad tracks all across the Sierras. They sometimes had to dig through solid granite in order to build a tunnel.

You would think that John McBride would have learned to appreciate the Huang brothers by now, for they had worked together on the transcontinental railroad twelve years before. They had helped finish that span in 1869. The last spike of the railroad had linked east to west, changing the United States forever.

Now, twelve years later, the brothers were in Colorado, helping McBride build hundreds of miles of track through impossible passes, such as this new 1,800-foot-long Alpine Tunnel. McBride and his dynamite blasters, Mike Doyle and Pat Ryan, seemed more hostile to the Huang brothers each day. McBride used every passing chance to harass the Chinese workers. He made cruel remarks and called them stupid because they still couldn't understand some English words. He called them heathens because they didn't share his faith, and he always tried to cheat them on payday.

Worse, McBride looked the other way when Mike and Pat played their so-called games. For example, whenever the two men set dynamite charges on the cliff, they tried to roll boulders down onto the Chinese workers, who were building snowsheds in the valley.

Mike's favorite game had only two rules. First, make sure that Mike and Pat are safe when they light the dynamite. Second, forget to give the warning shout to the Chinese. The winner was the one who counted the most Chinese running for their lives. McBride didn't mind. He didn't even care when a worker died. "We can get another one tomorrow," he said and shrugged.

Liu Huang, the oldest of the brothers, swore he would kill Mike and Pat someday. "I'll get McBride, too," he said. "They don't deserve to live."

Chih Huang, the middle brother, who had passed the civil service examination in his homeland, argued that they should be protected by United States law. "Surely, there should be justice here for everyone," he protested.

"There is no judge in this land who will protect us," said Tsun Huang, the youngest brother.

"Come, sing for us so that we can forget this cold," said Liu, turning to Tsun and laughing. "Your little songs will make our family famous." Liu pointed to Tsun's small drum. Tsun was an expert drummer. He carried his small drum to work, and on their rare breaks, he entertained the other Chinese workers with his songs.

Tsun frowned. "Please listen to me. Something is not right with the Alpine Tunnel. Last night, I walked up the ridge to look at the Big Dipper, and I noticed that the tunnel seems to cut it in half as the stars rise over the ridge. That is a bad omen. I have a feeling that our lives will change soon." He looked worried.

Liu laughed again. "Don't tell us that you believe in such things."

"I do believe in such things," Tsun murmured, as he blew out their small oil lamp. The three brothers settled down to sleep.

Liu dreamed of the day that he would seek revenge for the lives of all the Chinese who had been killed or hurt by their railroad bosses. Restlessly, Liu tossed from side to side in his bed. Tsun, in the next bunk, did not dream in pictures. Instead, he heard the steady beat of a *fa-ku* (a "drum of the law"), calling the monks to their temples at dawn. A stern voice repeated: "When the drum sounds, justice will come." Tsun woke early the next morning to the sound of a far-off drum. "What was that?" he mumbled, as he struggled to his feet. Did you hear anything, brothers?" Liu and Chih merely shook their heads, lit the lamp, and hurried into their clothes.

"We're late for work. Our friends are already on their way to the tunnel," Chih said. "We must hurry."

They shivered in the cold mountain air. At an altitude of 11,596 feet, the Alpine Pass discouraged even the most hearty laborers. The highest railroad pass in America, Alpine was plagued by high winds and blizzards. Most American workers refused to stay for more than a few days. Yet, the Chinese had been there since January of 1880, when construction began.

The morning sun warmed them as they trudged up the half-mile trail on the eastern slope of the ridge. "The wind has stopped, and it is quiet now. Perhaps the sun will begin to melt the ice on the rails," Liu remarked to Tsun, who walked next to him.

Tsun paid no attention. "Wait!" he said, "I forgot my drum." He turned back down the trail.

"You can't go back, we're too late," said Chih. "We will have to do without it."

The group of forty workers walked together down the eastern slope to begin another day of hard work. As they came around a curve in the trail, they saw Mike and Pat with Mr. McBride down in the distance to the north. The three men were near the bottom of the sheer rock wall, close to a snowshed. "They want to check above the snowshed to see if they can start work there. But what's Mr. McBride doing?" asked Chih.

154

"He's still trying to shoot an elk," said Liu. "He's been trying to get one all winter." They watched, as McBride aimed his rifle across the valley and shot into the trees. Liu smiled and then looked at Tsun, who was lost in thought. The group went on, wading through the heavy snow.

Suddenly, a sound echoed through the calm air. "The *fa-ku*! It's the drum of the law," gasped Tsun, "the same one that I heard this morning!"

"It's only McBride, shooting at shadows again," Liu said.

"Take cover!" yelled Chih. "He's started an avalanche!"

The sound of the avalanche, like distant thunder, seemed to last for hours. When it stopped, all the workers gathered together. No one was missing, but the outline of the ridge had changed. The avalanche had stripped branches from some tall fir trees, and other trees were completely buried.

"Where's the snowshed?" someone asked. "Where are Mike and Pat? Where's Mr. McBride?" another voice added.

"Forget them. The wind is picking up. We can't stay here any longer," Liu shouted. He tried to walk faster through the snow, away from the direction of the buried snowshed.

"If they heard the avalanche in time, they may have rushed to the shed. We must find them, Liu. It is our duty," said Tsun. He thought about the sound of the *fa-ku*, while he waited to hear Liu's reply.

"I hope that we don't see them until every drop of snow melts from this mountain and the rivers dry up. I hope that no one ever sees them again," Liu growled.

"If you are granted that wish, Liu, you will never again find peace," said Tsun quietly without looking at

155

his eldest brother. Turning, he spoke to a few men standing behind him. "We must go back for shovels, while Liu and Chih lead the search."

Liu hesitated, then snarled: "My brothers are right. It is our duty to search. Here, help me pull the rest of the branches from this pine tree. We can use it to dig. It will help us locate the snowshed and make an air hole." No one dared to argue with Liu. Everyone knew how much he hated the bosses and how his heart and mind were at war with each other. Many shared his conflict, and yet, under Liu's direction, they rushed to make the fallen trees and branches into digging poles— some as long as twenty feet. A giant juniper growing out of the rock wall served as a landmark. It led directly to the snowshed, which was buried three hundred feet below.

Within the hour, small groups of workers had spread out across the area above the snowshed. Each group began to bore into the snow. Liu was working feverishly on the heaviest pole, when Tsun and Chih returned with the tools. The search continued for another two hours. All the while, the cold wind blew around them. Another storm was approaching. Then, at eleven o'clock, they heard the sound that they had been waiting for: thud, thud, thud. Their poles had struck the snowshed roof that was buried in the snow beneath them. Even the tall smokestack was buried. "If they're in there, they can't last much longer," Liu said.

The brothers struck their pole once more and waited for a reply. By some miracle, Tsun could hear a faint response beating up from the hole in the snow. At least one man was alive, buried twenty feet below them. Racing against the storm, they dug an angular shaft. Then they began to tunnel down to the snowshed. The work seemed to take hours in freezing temperature, as

156

the sun moved to the west and the wind shifted to the north.

Just before the daylight began to fade, they dug through the roof. There was an open space under the shed that the snow had not filled. This had provided the men with some air. The diggers dropped a rope into the tunnel that they had created.

Somehow, they managed to pull Pat from the shed. His legs were broken, but he was still alive. Then Mike crawled out, a look of terror in his eyes. McBride was alive, too, but he was in shock. His eyes were open wide, staring at nothing.

"The drum, the drum," Tsun kept repeating as he looked at the men they had saved. He thought of the drum that was used to call the monks to their temples. It was the drum of justice. Now, magically, it had beat for them. But what was justice? he wondered. Was it the avalanche that had almost destroyed their enemies? Or was it the fact that he and his two brothers had worked to save them?

READING FOR UNDERSTANDING

1. Arrange the following incidents in the order in which they occurred:

    (a) Chih yelled for the men to take cover from the avalanche.

    (b) The diggers pulled Pat from the snowshed.

    (c) Tsun warned that something was wrong with the tunnel.

    (d) McBride shot his rifle across the valley.

    (e) Liu asked the men to help make digging poles.

2. What were some of the ways that John McBride and his blasters, Mike Doyle and Pat Ryan, abused the Chinese workers?

3. How were the attitudes of the three Huang brothers—Liu, Chih, and Tsun—quite different? Which brother seemed to be the most bitter about the treatment of the Chinese workers at the hands of their bosses?

4. Who received justice in this story? How was it carried out?

5. What caused the avalanche? Describe the results.

6. How do you think Liu and Tsun felt about having saved McBride, Doyle, and Ryan?

RESPONDING TO THE STORY

How did the end of this story make you feel about McBride and the two dynamite blasters, Mike and Pat? How did you feel about the three Huang brothers and their actions? Explain your reactions in a paragraph.

REVIEWING VOCABULARY

Match each word on the left with the correct definition on the right.

1. trudged
2. heathens
3. plagued
4. dynamite
5. harass
6. sheer

a. attack or bother
b. extremely steep
c. walked wearily
d. badly troubled
e. persons who do not believe in the God of the Bible
f. powerful explosive

THINKING CRITICALLY

1. What did the author tell you about the experiences of the Chinese workers in the western United States during the late nineteenth century? What was the bosses' attitude toward the Chinese? Why do you think that the Chinese were treated so unjustly?

2. What was Liu's main conflict in the story? How did Tsun's advice help Liu to stop seeking revenge? What did Liu do instead?

3. Should Liu have abandoned the bosses who tormented him and his people? Explain your opinion.

4. What does the story's title mean? By the end of the story, justice has been done. Is this your idea of justice? Why or why not?

5. In the first sentence of the story, we read that the Huang brothers "knew how to survive." How did the story support this statement?

Unit 5
PERSONAL
SURVIVAL

UNDER THE RUBBLE

Sandra Widener

Imagine you are in a room one bright, sunny day. Suddenly, without warning, the floor starts to shake. Furniture falls around you. Pictures fall off walls. Windows may even break. You are feeling an earthquake. It may last only a few moments, but an earthquake is something that you never forget.

Many people have experienced this scary situation. People in California, in particular, know what it's like. This is because large areas of the state lie over faults. Faults are cracks in the earth's surface. When the earth moves along these cracks, earthquakes occur.

The story that you are about to read takes place in a city in California. As you read, put yourself in Salaam's shoes. How would you feel if you were in his place? Find out how Salaam survives his first earthquake.

VOCABULARY WORDS

rummaged (RUM-ihjd) searched by moving things about

❖ She *rummaged* through her purse to find her keys.

confirm (kuhn-FERM) prove that something is true

❖ I gave him my license to *confirm* that I could drive.

condo (KAHN-doh) short for *condominium*, a building where each apartment is owned, not rented

❖ The young couple decided to buy the *condo*.

masonry (MAY-suhn-ree) brick work or stone work

❖ The roof of the temple was wooden, but the walls were made of *masonry*.

detached (dih-TACHT) not involved emotionally

❖ Even though her children were arguing, she remained *detached*.

paralyzed (PAR-uh-lyzd) unable to move or function

❖ After the car crash, she was *paralyzed* and needed a wheelchair.

rubble (RUB-uhl) broken pieces of a building

❖ All that remained of the bombed building was *rubble*.

debris (duh-BREE) broken bits and pieces

❖ After the hurricane, we sorted through the *debris*.

dire (DYR) dreadful; terrible

❖ When the river flooded over, it was a *dire* emergency.

**S**alaam propped his bike against the wall of the apartment building. He pulled the crumpled piece of paper out of his pocket and checked the address: 4235A Pine. The place should be here, he thought. He looked up at the door of a neat, modern apartment building but saw no number. Great, he thought to himself. Salaam tried the door of the main entrance and found it open. He rummaged around in his bag, got out the package that he was supposed to deliver, and went into the building.

"Hello? Hello?" he called. Since there was no answer, Salaam decided to walk down the corridor to the mail room. If there was some mail lying around, it would at least confirm the address.

He was stooped over, looking at some envelopes on the floor, when the first shock hit. It started as a slow rumble and got deeper and stronger. Salaam fell to the floor. He heard shattering, as dishes and glasses in the surrounding apartments crashed to the floor. He was on his hands and knees, with the world shaking around him. The wooden planks of the floor started to ripple as if Salaam were in the middle of the ocean, riding the waves.

It's the big one, Salaam thought in terror. It's the big one, and here I am, about to be buried alive in a condo. Slowly, trying to keep from being thrown into a wall, he crawled over to a door frame and held it. The frame strained and buckled in his hands.

When is this going to end? Salaam thought desperately. His ears were filled with a deafening roar. There was an endless shaking. It sounded like furniture being tossed around and pictures falling off walls in the apartments around and above him. Then Salaam heard a ripping sound overhead, a terrible noise that sounded as if the building were being torn in two. Plaster dust choked Salaam, as part of the ceiling came crashing down, leaving jagged pieces of masonry hanging above him. This is never going to end, thought Salaam in a detached, almost calm way. This is the end of the world. That was his last thought before another piece of the ceiling came hurtling down on his head and knocked him out.

When he regained consciousness, it was night. Everything was silent and dark. For an instant, Salaam panicked. He had no idea where he was. He felt a deep, aching pain in his legs. His head was pounding, his arms hurt, and he was lying in a puddle of water. Cautiously, he tried to move his legs, but they wouldn't

move. Why couldn't he move? Salaam's mind raced, as he thought: I am paralyzed—I am trapped. Could he feel his legs? He reached down and cautiously pinched a leg. Suddenly, he was flooded with relief because he had felt the pinch. His legs had feeling, therefore, they would be all right. He closed his eyes for several seconds to let this sink in.

Salaam didn't know what to do next. He had never been in an earthquake before. . . . It was so silent, so dark. Salaam wondered fearfully how his family was. Had his parents and sisters survived? Was his own house still standing? Was there anyone alive in the world?

"Hello," Salaam called feebly. He cleared his throat and tried again. This time his voice rang out as more of a shout, "Hello! Anybody here?" Only silence answered his cries.

Salaam began to make out shapes in the darkness. He could dimly see that his legs were buried beneath a pile of rubble. There was no way that he could move this pile. Feeling another wave of panic, he took a deep breath to calm himself.

Salaam was exhausted, as weary as he could ever remember being. He was also cold and frightened, and everything hurt. He was convinced that he was going to die here. Suddenly, Salaam was sobbing uncontrollably. He sobbed until he was drained of tears. Then he felt around, found a small piece of wall, and pulled it over to him. He put it underneath his head, twisted his body until he was on his side, and fell soundly asleep.

When Salaam woke up, it was morning. He still hurt everywhere. His legs were still the biggest problem. They were painful, but at least that meant they weren't paralyzed. He looked around, and, in the gray rays slanting through the jagged cracks of the walls, he could see the piles of rubble around him. He gasped when he saw the broken walls and twisted metal bars piled on top of his legs. How could he move that mass of material? You have to try, he told himself sternly. No one's coming to get you; no one knows where you are. You'll die in here unless you save yourself.

He was thirsty. He glanced down at the muddy water that he was lying in. Could he drink that? No, he wasn't that thirsty, not yet. What I need, Salaam thought, is a plan. Maybe the pile of rubble just looked impossible to move. If he worked steadily at it, a little at a time, he might be able to move it. In any case, he had to make an attempt. Above him, the debris was piled in a teetering heap so high that he had to study it to decide where to begin first. Straining, he pulled out a board, then another, and another. This is going to work, Salaam thought with mounting excitement. He began pulling out boards, clearing away debris, working quickly. As he pulled out a long board, he felt the pile shift. To his horror, he watched the pile wobble and then come crashing down on top of him. He put up his hands to shield himself as the debris landed on his head and chest. Then the dust rose silently.

Despairingly, Salaam closed his eyes. Now he was completely pinned by this new pile of rubble. He tried to move his arms and couldn't. Then, as if the situation were not dire enough, he felt an aftershock hit. In terror, Salaam watched helplessly, as more plaster and boards fell around him. The aftershock seemed to last an eternity. When it was finally over, he opened his eyes. This time, he cried silently, tears making tracks through the dust on his face—tracks he was unable to wipe away. Again, Salaam collapsed and slept.

Sometime later that day, he woke up again, hurting all over and so thirsty that his tongue felt like a piece of thick bread stuffed in his mouth. He could barely swallow. "Help," he tried to yell, but the sound was scratchy and small. He stared at the remains of the ceiling.

Outside, the sound of a siren blared. "Help," Salaam tried yelling again. No one answered. Then Salaam heard what sounded like voices from far away. "Help!" he screamed, gathering his strength into a cry so loud that his head felt like it would explode.

"What's that?" someone outside asked. Then someone else said: "Did you hear that? I think someone's in there."

"Help! In here!" Salaam cried, gathering his courage and his energy into a cry. "Help!"

"You're right! Someone's in there! I thought we'd searched this building. Didn't we search this building, Joe?" asked another voice. "Well, whether we did or not, someone's in there," said the other voice.

"I am in here! I am," Salaam cried.

"See? You hear that?" said the first man. "Well, get going," said the second.

Salaam heard scraping, pounding, the sounds of dragging. After another eternity, someone pulled back a heavy beam with difficulty. Salaam saw a face, a grinning, face whose expression turned to amazement when he spotted Salaam. Then the visitor whistled.

"Ooowee! Joe, get in here. We've got some digging to do." The brown face came into the room, attached to a long body dressed in muddy clothes. "You okay, buddy?" asked the brown man.

Salaam tried to smile but abandoned the effort. Instead, he nodded and then opened his parched lips to say, "Water."

The man looked concerned and answered, "Of course, of course," he said, pulling out a water bottle.

The man leaned over to Salaam and squirted the water directly into Salaam's open mouth. Salaam swallowed. Nothing had ever felt and tasted so good.

"Don't you worry. We'll get you out of here in no time," the man said. His partner entered the room, and the two began lifting debris off Salaam, talking to him reassuringly the whole time.

"That was some earthquake," the tall one said. "In a little while, we'll have you out of here," said the other, and then paused to punch some buttons on his mobile phone. "Janey? Get an ambulance over here: Pine and 42nd. We've got an injured person here." Then he grinned at Salaam and asked, "How do you feel?"

"Better," Salaam answered, but he was too tired to be witty, too tired for conversation. It was as if he suddenly could relax, let the pain take over, let someone else worry, go limp.

After a few more minutes, the two men had freed Salaam. His legs were battered, but he could still feel them. The two men gently carried him out and placed him onto the stretcher brought by the ambulance. The ambulance lights were flashing in the street, lighting up tired, worried faces and jagged walls. "Don't worry," said a man with a white shirt, patting Salaam's elbow. "It's going to be all right."

Salaam didn't answer the man because his mind was elsewhere. He was thinking about the package that he had been sent to deliver to 4235A Pine. He suddenly realized that no one had signed for it. Salaam hoped that everything would be okay.

READING FOR UNDERSTANDING

The paragraph below summarizes the story. Decide which of the words below the paragraph best fits each blank. Write your answers on a separate sheet of paper.

Salaam was in the condo because he was trying to **(1)**_____ a **(2)**_____. Suddenly an **(3)**_____ started to **(4)**_____ everything around him. Part of the **(5)**_____ crashed down on top of him and he was **(6)**_____ out. When he came to, he first thought that he was paralyzed, but then felt **(7)**_____ to find that his legs had **(8)**_____. He was **(9)**_____ beneath a pile of rubble, and he finally decided that he had to try to **(10)**_____ himself. But after he pulled out a few **(11)**_____, the pile **(12)**_____ down on top of him and he couldn't move his arms or **(13)**_____. Later, after waking up, he heard **(14)**_____ and **(15)**_____ for help. Two men came and, after digging, were able to free Salaam.

Words: *boards, buried, ceiling, crashed, deliver, earthquake, happy, knocked, legs, package, save, screamed, shake, voices, feeling*

RESPONDING TO THE STORY

Did you ever think that you might be trapped somewhere? Perhaps it was a bathroom door that wouldn't open or an elevator that stopped between floors. Or maybe it was just a feeling. Write a brief description of the situation. Make your reader "feel" what is happening.

REVIEWING VOCABULARY

1. If I am looking for a *condo*, I want to **(a)** buy a place to live **(b)** stay at a friend's house **(c)** rent an apartment.

2. An example of *debris* is **(a)** groceries in a paper bag **(b)** ingredients to make a meal **(c)** garbage in the street.

3. A *detached* person would be likely to **(a)** get angry very easily **(b)** stay calm in an argument **(c)** cry during a fight.

4. In a *dire* situation, people are **(a)** bored **(b)** upset **(c)** happy.

5. If I *confirm* that I'll be late, I **(a)** won't arrive on time **(b)** might arrive on time **(c)** won't arrive late.

6. You'd see *rubble* after **(a)** rain **(b)** snow **(c)** a tornado.

7. If I *rummaged* through my closet, I was probably **(a)** looking for something **(b)** measuring it **(c)** vacuuming it.

THINKING CRITICALLY

1. The story maintained suspense by letting the reader discover things slowly. For example, Salaam first thought that his legs might be paralyzed, then found that they weren't. How would you rewrite this story to make it even more suspenseful?

2. What kind of person is Salaam? Why do you think that the author ended the story with Salaam's thinking about the package that he was sent to deliver? Support your opinion with examples from the story.

RIVER RUN

David Irland

Have you ever been in a kayak or a canoe on a fast-flowing river? Have you ever seen salmon heading upstream in the springtime? Tulee, the elderly Native American hero of this story, has spent his whole life out-doors. He has always lived surrounded by nature's beauty in the Pacific Northwest. Tulee is proud of his Yakima Indian roots. His upbringing helps him to survive a life-and-death threat when he suddenly meets up with poachers on the Yakima River.

The poachers are younger than Tulee, and they are armed. Tulee is a retired ranger. Chasing poachers is the work of younger men. But Tulee has a responsibility to his people. He still feels that he must uphold the law. He knows that his knowledge of the river can help him.

VOCABULARY WORDS

kayak (KY-ak) a type of canoe
❖ I rented a *kayak* for a trip on the river.

flotation (floh-TAY-shuhn) allowing an object to float
❖ Fiberglass is a *flotation* material used in many small boats.

poachers (POHCH-erz) people engaged in illegal hunting or fishing
❖ Forest rangers often find it hard to protect endangered wildlife from *poachers*.

spawning (SPAWN-ihng) breeding
❖ That year, fewer salmon than normal returned to their usual *spawning* grounds.

ancestral (an-SEHS-truhl) inherited from ancestors
❖ The Yakima Indians were proud of their *ancestral* customs.

vise (VYS) device used on a workbench to hold an object
❖ My leg, pinned by the rocks, felt as if it were in a *vise*.

booty (BOOT-ee) prize or spoils seized by force
❖ The pirates were pleased at the *booty* that they collected on their raid.

fragrant (FRAY-gruhnt) sweet-smelling
❖ In the garden, we noticed the *fragrant* scent of the roses.

KEY WORD

Yakima (YAK-uh-muh) river and Native American tribe in the state of Washington
❖ Last summer, we went canoeing on the *Yakima* River.

Today, **the Yakima River,** which is in the state of Washington, was covered with leaves and twigs. It was spring runoff time. All the recent snow had melted. It had flowed down from the mountains, carrying the leaves and twigs with it. The river was fast today. It made a loud, rushing sound. Tulee felt happy to be out in his kayak again. It had been such a long winter. He watched the salmon racing upstream. The salmon reminded him of the day that he had retired as a river ranger. Chief Smohalla had wished him "good health" and had handed him some small, carved pieces of wood, which looked like a set of car keys. But instead of a new car, there on the fall leaves sat one of the best available Class II white water kayaks. Tulee's wife, Taswatha, stood proudly to one side, her face grinning with happiness.

Tulee paddled hard against the rushing water. Then he stopped, forcing the paddle deep. He was about to try one of his specialties, an "Eskimo roll." You did it by leaning suddenly to one side so that the kayak flipped over. You dunked your head, shoulders, and body, then flipped upright again. But before Tulee could try the trick, a salmon leaped out of the water and landed on the kayak. It was a large sockeye salmon. The big eye stared at him. The huge hook-jaw slammed open and then slammed closed.

"Be gone, big friend!"

Tulee gently pushed the fish back into the river.

"Best of luck on your long journey," he told the fish.

During his days as a river ranger, Tulee had made sure that only his people could fish in this river. The river had belonged to the Yakima Indians long before the coming of the white people. The U.S. government had made a law saying that the fish belonged to the Indians alone.

Suddenly, Tulee heard a strange noise. It just didn't fit into the natural sounds of the river, rocks, and trees. He got worried for a second but then scolded himself.

"Calm down, fool! Probably an old raccoon, thinking about a salmon lunch."

He squinted at the shore. He saw low branches springing back into place. Something large had moved them aside. Gliding with the fast current, Tulee angled the boat until he felt the bottom of it touch the shore. He got out and tugged the almost weightless hull onto the beach with one hand. On the beach were fresh jeep tracks showing fat flotation tires.

"Poachers," he said aloud to himself.

Tulee knew that the spawning season attracted poachers. They were people who fished illegally and then sold the fish for profit. Poaching was against the law. It deprived the Yakima Indians of their ancestral fishing privileges. The tribe had fished along this river for centuries. A treaty with the U.S. government still guaranteed their exclusive right to fish here. Tulee had trapped many poachers as a ranger. But now he was retired! He looked down at his wrinkled hands. He didn't have to chase criminals anymore, did he?

The river ranger inside Tulee pushed the boat toward the water. He leaped in and moved away from the shore with a powerful stroke of his paddle. Carving his way through the bulging water, he poked through a white fountain of foam. Old habits came back. He reached out and swerved the boat away from an approaching rock. Perfect. Danger was near, but he grinned. He focused on keeping level, just like in the old days. The roar of water was in his ears. The sun was out, and the shore looked jagged and clean.

A line of round orange floats interrupted his vision. Stretched tight across the river was a stout line holding up an illegal net. He'd found the poachers' secret. The net would catch the salmon as they swam upstream.

Suddenly, a man holding a rifle stepped into the clearing to Tulee's left. Without having to think about it, Tulee shifted his hips to the side. The boat flipped upside down. Tulee's body felt the cold of the water. Underwater, the roar of the river became a hush. Bubbles rose, bouncing across his still-open eyes.

Through the water, he heard a muffled sound like a stick snapping beneath a pillow. Then he saw the thin, white jet stream of a bullet piercing the clear water. His lungs felt tight, as if his whole chest were being crushed in a vise. The whole world slowed. There was no way that he could stay underwater any longer. With a jerk of his body, the kayak flipped right-side-up again.

The world up above was cool, crisp, and much noisier. Skimming the shore, Tulee balanced on the clear water. To his left, rocks made the river impassable. To his right, framed in the trees, staring at him, was an angry, bearded face that he would never forget. It was the man with the gun.

Tulee was in a trap. His truck was waiting in a wide, clear meadow. But he was like a tin duck in a shooting gallery. How could he escape? In his mind, he saw the river from Prosser to Benton City, everything that he'd ever known about it. It stood out clearly like a map. He formed a plan.

Tulee began paddling furiously as three bullets whizzed by him. The kayak sped silently into a narrow, rocky inlet. The hull slipped, crunched, but shot ahead. Ducking beneath a branch, he found what he needed.

Under the tangled branches of some trees was a shaded pool of cool, calm water—a deep hole that

175

trout loved. It was just as he remembered from years ago. He'd spent many carefree summer days fishing there, catching not just salmon but trout.

At the far end of the pool was another narrow opening. Tulee raced toward it, following the mossy banks. A hush filled the space behind him, as the rushing river faded away. In the faraway distance, a poacher's truck horn hooted. Another poacher's horn, angrier, hooted back.

Tulee made very good progress. He knew this winding water trail well. He knew he could use this indirect route as a shortcut and wind up much farther down river.

Soon, he was back on the fast-flowing Yakima. His breath came easier now. He hoped that the poachers were still at their nasty game. He'd bob down the river calmly and report the poachers to the Kiona River Base rangers. The rest would be left in the hands of younger men, men with their careers ahead of them.

Tulee's attention was caught by a noise. It was similar to the one that he'd heard underwater, only clearer. He shortened his stroke. He looked around. That sound was another shot. The race was on. He had to reach the ranger base before the poachers got him. In the distance, he could see the poachers' trucks moving along the shore in quick bursts, barreling over tree stumps.

Tulee felt as if he were fifteen again, a young man. He paddled with that automatic rhythm of someone who has grown up on the river. These were the same rapids that he'd traveled when his father, Teio, had been mauled by a bear and needed help. Thoughts of salmon, men, and bears drifted through his mind.

The rhythm of his paddling was subtly changing. He was moving more smoothly now. His upper body began to relax.

Tulee's strokes seemed to understand what was ahead. The Squawfish Falls made the wildness of the rest of the Yakima River seem gentle by comparison. He saw the falls from fifty feet and then from twenty. Directly ahead, the drop was as high as two kayaks placed end to end. He saw the picture in his head like a photograph from a long time ago. That time he'd survived. And he would again. He would soar over the falls. The salmon did; the eagles did.

Lifting a little, the kayak soared over the edge. Afloat in the air full of spray, Tulee could see only white boiling water below, blue sky above. The little bean pod with the man in it dropped like a stone.

Beneath any falls, the water is very deep. The falling water pushes the bottom down, hollowing it out over time. As he plunged into that wilderness of cold water, Tulee was aware of pressure in his ears. It was deep-water pressure. Then, finally, the kayak began to rise.

Still numb, Tulee began to act. His hips twisted and turned; the bow lifted. Instinct and years of racing rapids came to help him. He did the correct things, despite the freezing cold and the water's pressure. He used his hips to aim the kayak at the light, at the blue daylight. The kayak became a missile and headed for the surface. Finally, the boat pierced the surface and bobbed up, shedding water.

Tulee's eyes popped open. First, he saw the bow of the kayak. Reedy river-bottom mud hung from the beautifully pointed tip.

Tulee rested in the green cave behind the falls. He bobbed on the surface, inches from the sheet of falling water. Quiet and still, he waited in the fragrant air.

When he finally emerged, he realized that the woods were now silent. There were no guns firing and no truck engines roaring. There was only the sound of the falls, reaching up into the hills and echoing back. The poachers were nowhere to be seen. They were probably gathering their live, squirming booty from the net. But they were probably also attracting a lot of attention.

He pictured the Forest Service helicopter. He imagined it buzzing in circles, sweeping the spiky green trees. He saw the white cone of its lights shining on the poachers. He wouldn't get a medal this time. But he had used his Native American skills to outwit them. He had led them toward the ranger base while escaping them. The river still felt like his own, a friend for life.

READING FOR UNDERSTANDING

1. Tulee was a retired **(a)** policeman **(b)** fire chief **(c)** river ranger.

2. In a maneuver called the "Eskimo roll," a kayak **(a)** rocks from side to side **(b)** goes over a waterfall **(c)** is flipped over and then is flipped upright.

3. We can assume from the story that Tulee **(a)** was proud of the Yakimas' rights to fish the river **(b)** had a chip on his shoulder against the poachers **(c)** was unhappy in retirement.

4. Tulee used a shortcut because **(a)** his kayak needed repairs **(b)** he would get tired otherwise **(c)** he had to reach the ranger base quickly.

5. From the end of the story, we can assume that **(a)** Tulee would return to active duty **(b)** the poachers would be caught **(c)** the poachers would escape.

RESPONDING TO THE STORY

What impression did Tulee make on you? Would you like to have him as a friend or teacher? In a paragraph, describe what you think Tulee is like. Include your reactions to him.

REVIEWING VOCABULARY

The following sentences are based on the story. Decide which of the words following the sentences best fits each blank. Write your answers on a separate sheet of paper.

1. Tulee was happy to be in his _____.

2. Fresh tracks of fat _____ tires were on the beach.

3. Poaching deprived the Yakima of _____ fishing rights.

4. Tulee's chest felt as if it were squeezed in a _____.

5. Breathing the _____ air, Tulee rested in a grotto.

6. The salmon were in their _____ season.

7. Endangered wildlife is further threatened by _____.

8. They were taking the live _____ from the net.

Words: *ancestral, booty, flotation, fragrant, kayak, poachers, spawning, vise*

THINKING CRITICALLY

1. In this story, Tulee was presented as a man very much in tune with nature. For example, early in the story, he released the salmon that jumped into his kayak, calling the fish "big friend" and wishing it good luck on its long journey. What are other ways in which the writer showed that Tulee was in harmony with nature?

2. How did Tulee's understanding of nature help him survive when he was threatened by poachers?

3. What do you think Tulee might have said to the poachers about their behavior? How would he have explained his people's right to be the only ones to fish in the river?

HOME BY DARK

Carroll Moulton

People who live in the United States are lucky. Not since the Civil War has a war been fought on U.S. soil. Imagine a war right in your own city or town, with battles going on all around your home! Consider what effects this would have on your everyday life.

This story is about a boy whose country is torn apart by war. Like all children, he loves to play. But his innocent game of soccer is soon replaced by a more dangerous adventure that could cost him his life.

As you will see, battlefields are not always in remote areas, and war is a terrible experience for those who must live in the middle of them. The story is set in an unnamed Middle Eastern country on the Mediterranean, a sea that touches Europe, Africa, and Asia.

VOCABULARY WORDS

barren (BAR-uhn) having little or no vegetation
❖ He will never grow anything on that *barren* land.

bougainvillea (bou-guhn-VIHL-ee-uh) a tropical vine
❖ The *bougainvillea* vine had large, purple flowers.

volleys (VAHL-eez) many weapons going off at once
❖ The *volleys* of gunfire echoed into the night.

cease-fire (SEES-FYR) temporary stopping of battle
❖ The *cease-fire* lasted only until dawn.

curfew (KER-fyoo) period of time to be at home and not on the streets
❖ I asked my parents for a later *curfew*.

reinstated (ree-ihn-STAY-tuhd) put back to a previous condition
❖ The fired professor was *reinstated* after a student protest.

violators (VY-uh-lay-tuhrz) those who break a rule or law
❖ She believed that all *violators* should be punished.

gorge (GAWRJ) a deep, narrow valley
❖ Looking down into the *gorge* made me very dizzy.

ascent (uh-SEHNT) act of going up
❖ Our *ascent* to the top of the mountain took all day.

descent (dih-SEHNT) act of coming down
❖ On her *descent* to the bottom of the sea, she saw many beautiful fish.

**All afternoon,** under a glaring Mediterranean sun, they played soccer. The teams were missing players—only seven players on one side and six on the other. The field was an oddly shaped patch of barren ground near the port, littered with chalky rubble. But these eleven- and twelve-year-olds played the game as seriously as if it were a match for the World Cup.

His team had chosen him to play goalie, and he had prevented two penalty kicks from scoring. After the game, he walked to his friend's house, where he had left his knapsack. His friend patted him on the back.

"You were the reason we won!" he said.

The boy smiled, trying not to look too proud. They turned into the gate of a small villa, where red and purple bougainvillea splashed color on the high, white-washed walls around a courtyard.

It was just then that the boy and his friend heard the gunfire. One burst of shots, which sounded quite far off, was followed by three longer, closer volleys. The cease-fire had lasted only a week. It was just long enough for the people of the boy's town to take one sigh of relief. Then the ugly battle had started up again.

"Stay the night here," the boy's friend said. "There'll be a curfew now, you know."

The boy shook his head. "No, I must get home."

"You'd better hurry then."

The boy nodded, grabbed his knapsack, and quickly stepped back into the street. He looked at the setting sun: fifteen minutes till sunset and then a half hour of twilight at most. He had three-quarters of an hour to get home by dark.

The boy lived in the old quarter of the city, straight across to the east, high up in the twisting streets near

183

the old fort. He lived in a tiny apartment with his mother and his three-year-old sister. Ever since the death of his father, who had fought on the side of the rebels in the civil war, he had been the man of the house.

The boy half ran, half walked. The first part of his route lay along one of the city's main avenues, which was now nearly deserted. Suddenly, a government army truck wheeled around a corner. Its loudspeaker was blaring the announcement that the curfew had been reinstated and that all citizens had to be off the streets by dark. Violators would be shot on sight.

The boy turned off the avenue and headed toward a steep side street that climbed eastward to the highway. This was the route that he would take to cross the gorge. Panting a little, the boy turned his head. He saw that he had climbed far enough to glimpse the bay, which the oncoming night was turning from blue to purple.

Home by dark, he thought. I should just make it.

But when he reached the highway, he saw that the police checkpoints had already been set up. Soldiers were stopping what little traffic there was. He watched as flashing red lights glimmered in the dusk. A siren wailed in the distance.

To cross the gorge in plain sight was out of the question. Although the curfew was not yet technically in force, they would still stop him. They would ask him his name. He would lie, of course. If he told them his name, they would know that his father had been one of the rebels who fought against them. But even if he didn't, he had no way of knowing whether they would detain him or for how long.

There were only two other routes that he could take. He could backtrack down to the port and go all the way around by the sea. It would take hours, and he wouldn't get home till midnight, if then. Or he could leave the highway, slip through the tangles of barbed wire, and cross the gorge on foot. This way was also dangerous. For three years, since the beginning of the war, the gorge had been strewn with land mines and old, unexploded shells. But if he could get through the wire without being seen and pick his way through the mines, he'd be home by dark. He thought of his mother and sister, and decided that he would have to chance it.

Getting past the checkpoint unseen was easier than he'd expected. The police were busy with the driver of a fuel truck and did not notice him scrambling under the wire about a hundred feet away from the road. Because the gorge was steeply sloped, he was able to dig his sneakers deep into the gravel to keep his footing. The sneakers had been made in the United States, a gift from his friend's family. He thought briefly of the soccer game. Maybe he should have spent the night at his friend's home, after all.

Scrambling downward, it occurred to him that his greatest risk would be at the bottom of the gorge. He could see the fifty yards of level ground down there before the ascent to the far rim. He paused for a moment and tried to remember everything that he'd heard about mines. His father had warned him once about the deadly little traps that could blow your foot off in a puff of smoke. They were set off by trip wires, thin little wires close to the ground. These wires were almost impossible to see among the garbage and rubble at the bottom of the gorge.

The boy looked around. For the first time that day, he knew that he was afraid. His thin shirt clung wetly to him, both from the humid air of nightfall and from the effort of his descent, but most of all from fear.

185

And then he saw them: five, six—no, eight or nine dogs, scavenging in the area. The boy stared as the animals sniffed the ground. The dogs were big, some of them as heavy as he was. The boy had heard of packs of dogs, crazed by hunger, that had attacked young children, but these dogs seemed to take little interest in him. As they moved away from him, he watched them curiously. How did they get enough to eat? he wondered. How did they know where to step? Why didn't they get blown up?

Suddenly, it dawned on him that he would be safe if he followed the dogs' trail. Whether or not they could smell the mines, they all knew where the little wires were hidden. They would show him the way.

The boy studied the dogs' movements. It took him

186

nearly fifteen minutes to piece together a zigzag course across the fifty yards. He heard another spatter of gunfire in the distance. Then, from the great mosque near the fort, there drifted the notes of the evening call to prayer. The boy and his family were not formally religious, but now he had a prayer to offer. He prayed to get home.

Having crossed the rubble field, the boy started up the slope. He started to move faster, less concerned about mines. Finally, he burst up to the rim, dashing across the highway just before the floodlights blazed on. Up, up the hill toward the fort he ran, and then, heart racing now, he came to his own building. He rushed up the stairs to the apartment and pushed open the door.

His mother sat feeding his sister in the lamplight. He could tell that she had heard the gunfire and was frightened for him. She tried not to let her fear show.

"How was the game?" she asked, trying hard to sound matter-of-fact.

He smiled, still out of breath. "We won," was all he answered. Mother and son read each other perfectly. Both had to face each day with tremendous courage, without making a big deal out of it. In their hearts, both were well aware of the tragedy of war.

READING FOR UNDERSTANDING

1. Where did the boy go after the soccer game?
2. Why did the boy feel that it was important to go home rather than stay at his friend's house?
3. Why couldn't the boy be on the street after dark?
4. How was he able to get past the checkpoint?
5. What clue did the story give about the boy's religion?
6. Why do you think that his mother did not want to let her fear show?
7. What did the boy mean when he said "We won" at the end of the story? Was he talking only about the soccer game?

RESPONDING TO THE STORY

At the beginning of this story, the boy's friend invited him to stay over. But he decided to take his chances and try to get home. Have you ever taken a risk to accomplish something? Describe what it was. Tell how it turned out.

REVIEWING VOCABULARY

Match each word on the left with the correct definition on the right.

1. ascent	**a.** temporary stopping of battle
2. barren	**b.** not able to produce much
3. cease-fire	**c.** act of going up
4. curfew	**d.** deep, narrow valley
5. descent	**e.** many weapons going off at once
6. gorge	**f.** act of coming down
7. reinstated	**g.** put back to a previous condition
8. violators	**h.** period of time to be at home and not on the streets
9. volleys	**i.** those who break a rule or law
10. bougainvillea	**j.** tropical vine

THINKING CRITICALLY

1. The story does not have many specific details about the city, what the war was about, or even the name of the boy. Why do you think the author chose to leave these details out? What do you think the author was trying to say about the effects of war?

2. At the beginning of the story, a group of boys played soccer "as seriously as if it were a match for the World Cup." What does this statement tell you about the boys?

3. Why do you think there was a curfew? Why do you think it was enforced so strictly?

INTREPID

Joyce Haines

Some people don't know the meaning of the word quit. *In the story that you are about to read, Beth Perkins is a long-distance runner who has lost a leg to cancer. She doesn't sit back and feel sorry for herself, however. Far from it. Despite many problems and her parents' worries, Beth meets the challenge. She goes on a coast-to-coast walk to help change people's attitudes about persons with disabilities.*

In her travels, Beth encounters situations that tax both her mental and physical endurance. Just when it seems as if she's hit bottom, she makes some new friends who have a big problem of their own. As you read this story, think about how much effort you would give for a cause in which you strongly believe.

VOCABULARY WORDS

intrepid (ihn-TREHP-ihd) bold, fearless
❖ She faced challenges and hardships with an *intrepid* spirit.

marathons (MAR-uh-thahnz) 26.2-mile foot races
❖ *Marathons* are difficult to run, even if you're in top shape.

trek (TREHK) journey
❖ The *trek* of two thousand miles would take six months.

remission (rih-MIHSH-uhn) lessening or disappearance of the symptoms of a disease
❖ Some cancer patients experience *remission* and can lead normal lives.

gawk (GAWK) stare stupidly
❖ When people in cars slow down to *gawk* at accidents, they create dangerous conditions.

prosthesis (prahs-THEE-sihs) artificial body part
❖ More than one *prosthesis* might be needed for the journey.

ravine (ruh-VEEN) long, deep hole in the ground
❖ A marker separated the roadside from a deep *ravine*.

averted (uh-VERT-uhd) prevented, avoided
❖ A major disaster was *averted* because of the warning.

retrieve (rih-TREEV) get back, recover
❖ Greg dropped his glasses in the pool but was able to *retrieve* them.

comrades (KAHM-radz) friends, companions
❖ All my old *comrades* came to the school reunion.

It wasn't the cold that bothered Beth Perkins. She could always put on another sweater under her coat. Her new down tent and sleeping bag were the best that money could buy. Both were made to keep out the coldest Arctic air. So, the many nights that she spent between towns weren't as bad as people thought. In fact, she loved camping out in faraway places. She loved being in nature even more than she loved sports.

The rain didn't bother her, either. Beth wanted publicity, of course. Still, she was glad when bad weather kept the large crowds away. More and more people seemed to follow her through the cities. Reporters swarmed around the tall, young woman with the long, blonde hair. They always asked the same questions. "Aren't you afraid of walking by yourself?" . . . "How does your family feel about your trip?" . . . "Will you ever take up white-water rafting again?" . . . "Did you ever consider making your journey in a wheelchair?" . . . "Do you get imaginary pains in the knee and leg that you lost?" . . . "Do you miss your marathons?" . . . "Will you write a book?"

She didn't understand why they couldn't focus on the real issues. "Why can't people realize that people with disabilities have special strengths and abilities as well as needs? Don't we deserve equal employment opportunities? Can't our access to public buildings be improved? Why don't the laws address these issues?" She had been trying to get this message across long before she began her trek six months ago, on her twenty-first birthday. Sometimes, it seemed hopeless. However, Beth was convinced that her coast-to-coast walk would change people's attitudes. She just wished that she didn't have to make so many speeches.

"They call me 'intrepid,'" she thought to herself one night as she camped along the Little Miami River, just outside Dayton, Ohio. "They don't know that, for me, the trek is the easy part. It's speaking in public, in front of large crowds, that's difficult."

One of Beth's role models had always been Jane Goodall, who fought to save chimpanzees in Africa. Goodall herself once said that she would rather be attacked by a wild animal than speak in public. Yet, when the time came for her to speak, Goodall faced an audience and won support for her cause. Beth's feeling now was, "If Jane could do it, so can I."

By now, Beth had perfected the simple speech that she gave to civic groups along the way. She patiently told them about the cancer that had attacked the bone in her upper right leg. She explained the operation that had been necessary to remove her cancerous limb. She discussed remission. She tried to reach each member of the audience as an individual.

"I am here on behalf of thousands of physically challenged people just like me. I'm not here to ask for your money or your sympathy. The food and shelter that you've shared with me is enough. If my words move you to give something, then please give to the cancer research fund of your choice. But I am not asking you to give anything at all. No. Instead, I'm urging you to accept the good work that people with disabilities have to offer you. They are people who want to do an honest day's work for an honest wage, people who just need a chance. Look around your town. Please open your doors and your hearts to others like me."

The tears in the eyes of some listeners told Beth that they heard her message. She believed that they would try to get their employers to give jobs and opportunities to people with disabilities. Their promises helped her endure the pain of the long miles between towns.

She was glad that it was against the law to walk along the interstate highway. The roar of semi-trailer trucks, combined with exhaust fumes, could have been unbearable. It was true that frequent rest stops and telephones would have been useful. But she preferred the smaller, back country roads. There, she could walk in peace, enjoy the view, and enjoy the fresh air as she pushed the cart that held her gear and a sign: "Respect People with Disabilities."

To distract herself from the pain in her hip joints and the blisters on her left foot, Beth took pictures and thought about her family. She could still hear their words when she first told them about her plan. "Are you out of your mind?" her father screamed. More gently, her mother added, "Beth, do you think that this is safe? The doctor says that you've won the battle against cancer. You don't want to risk hurting yourself now." Her father's face was growing redder by the moment. "What about your plans to go to law school someday? You don't have time to walk across the country!"

Beth tried to see her parents' point of view. She was their only child. Since her illness, they had grown used to worrying about her. Now, she had been in remission for three years, and she knew that she had to help others. "This trip's not for me, Mom. Please understand . . . Dad, I still plan to go to law school. But first I have to make this journey. Don't you see? My trek could do more than any law to change the way that people look at physically challenged people. You know that, Dad."

Her father made one last attempt. "Why can't you just have one of those 5-K walks that people are always holding to increase public awareness?"

Beth tried to explain. "Those walks for special causes are great. But they hardly make the news. I want to

194

do something that will make a lasting impression. That's why I have to walk coast-to-coast. Besides, you know that I hate crowds. I can't stand it when people gawk at me. But I have to let them know that people with disabilities are capable people." In the end, Beth managed to convince them that her cause was worth it.

From that day forward, both her father and her mother began making extensive plans to help her. Beth didn't want to disappoint either one of them, but she told them that this had to be a solitary journey. What's more, Beth didn't want them to see the sores that she would get as she made her trek. Such a walk could never be easy, even for someone with both legs in working order. She anticipated blisters, calluses, and muscle pains in addition to problems caused by the weather. Beth's doctor made arrangements for her at clinics along the route that she planned to take. "The strongest prosthesis simply cannot hold up like a human leg does," he told her. Then he added that she should expect to need several replacements before the trip was over.

"Mom, Dad, I promise to call you often. And who knows? You may see me on TV, and I'll take lots of pictures with my new camera."

That conversation now seemed like a lifetime ago. Since Beth had left Jamestown, Virginia, six months ago, she had traveled more than a thousand miles and had made dozens of speeches. She had gone through twenty rolls of film, five left shoes, and countless bandages. She had also replaced one prosthesis and was ready for another new one. Beth's left leg and lower back ached constantly. With the extra time that she spent on medical exams, speeches, and camping in record-breaking rainfalls, Beth was lucky to cover about six miles a day. Weeks behind schedule, she also had to spend time calling people who were expecting her to tell them that she was going to be late.

Another month passed slowly. She was now down to five miles a day, but she had made it through St. Louis. All her waterproof gear was soaking wet from storms. Not even her yellow rubber raincoat could keep out all the water. Then Beth learned that the National Guard was preparing for the worst flood in a century. Several civic groups sent word that they had to cancel her speeches because of the floods in their areas. Beth realized that she would have to stop somewhere and wait out the storm.

First, Beth took a break at a rest stop on the outskirts of St. Charles, Missouri. She telephoned her parents to assure them that all was reasonably well. "I'm okay. I know I can make it. I've been walking on the main roads to avoid high water. I promise to call you later tonight from St. Charles. They have a place for me to stay there. Yes, that's the historic town on the river. I think that I may spend a few days there so I can rest up." She didn't want to mention the seriousness of the flooding or the new blisters that had started to appear on her foot.

After she hung up the telephone, Beth had to force herself back into the rainy day. It was only 10:00 A.M., yet the dark clouds made it look like night. She could barely see the red flag on her cart. She was still three long miles away from the house in St. Charles. Beth had never felt this tired in her life. It was only the thought of a warm meal, a hot bath, and a dry bed that kept her going.

"Hey, lady, you're limping. Do you want a ride? You look pretty wet," a stranger shouted as he drove past her in the parking lot. "No, thanks," Beth said, "I'm okay." Twenty minutes later, Beth was all alone on the

196

road that descended into the town. She kept close to the yellow mile markers which separated the right side of the road from a deep ravine.

Suddenly, a gush of water swept Beth off her feet, and she lost her grip on her cart. Dazed, she pulled herself up and saw that her raincoat was torn and her arm was bleeding slightly. But her legs were unhurt. "My tent and sleeping bag! My camera! Where's my camera?" She then saw that her cart had been swept down a ten-foot embankment.

Beth knew better than to try to maneuver down the muddy slope by herself. She needed help. After looking for a landmark so that she could remember the spot, she walked on. "It can't get much worse," she moaned. "Why did I ever try this? How can I go on?" Still, she kept walking.

As she came around a curve, she could finally see St. Charles. Long lines of people were passing sandbags down towards the river. They were too busy to pay attention to Beth's condition. "Hurry up, lady. We can use another pair of hands. Here, grab this bag."

Without speaking, she joined the line. Her gear would have to wait. No one stared at her. No one asked questions. No one doubted that she could do the job.

The crowd worked for hours. Once in a while, someone would relieve a worker for the few minutes that it took to grab a cup of hot coffee. The volunteers always came back without complaining. Their commitment to the job was something that Beth hadn't seen since she'd left the clinic that helped her learn to walk again. The sight of people working together for a common cause raised her spirits in spite of the rising river. This was an experience that she would never forget.

Finally, near midnight, the task was complete. A major flood had been averted. People were starting to return to their homes. Beth walked over to the group leader and told her story. The name and address of her hosts for the night were lost. She didn't know where to go. She could barely move.

"Do you mean to say you've been working here all day with only one good leg? . . . You walked all the way from Virginia?" he stammered. "Hey, Mayor. Come over here. You've got to meet this lady," the group leader called.

That night, and for a week afterward, Beth stayed in the mayor's home, resting. For the first 48 hours, she barely woke up to eat. In her dreams, she debated with herself over whether or not to give up the trek. On the third day, she finally woke up long enough to think about how the people stacking sandbags against the flood just wouldn't give up. Beth felt a kinship with these people. In fact, Beth now felt connected to everyone whom she had met on her trek. She saw the caring behind all those questions.

By some miracle, the mayor's husband had managed to retrieve and repair Beth's cart. He also made a new sign that read: "Intrepid Traveler."

Now Beth was ready to continue her trip. She was happy to discover that she no longer minded the crowds and the questions. She didn't even mind their stares. Recognizing her comrades from the night of the rising river, Beth waved and smiled as she walked uphill, toward the Pacific.

READING FOR UNDERSTANDING

1. The hardest thing for Beth was **(a)** getting enough sleep **(b)** dealing with pain **(c)** speaking in public.

2. Beth disliked reporters' questions because they always focused on physically challenged peoples' **(a)** families rather than on them **(b)** weaknesses rather than on their rights **(c)** dreams rather than on their realities.

3. In her speeches, Beth **(a)** quoted Jane Goodall **(b)** asked for money **(c)** tried to reach all listeners.

4. Beth's journey had to be solitary in order to **(a)** prove to her parents that she could make it alone **(b)** give her some time to be by herself **(c)** show that physically challenged people could be independent.

5. In St. Charles, Missouri, Beth helped a crowd of volunteers to prevent a(n) **(a)** fire **(b)** flood **(c)** epidemic.

6. The mayor's husband managed to retrieve Beth's **(a)** cart **(b)** backpack **(c)** winter jacket.

RESPONDING TO THE STORY

One of Beth's role models was Jane Goodall. Who are your role models, and what do they mean to you? Write a diary entry explaining whom you admire and why.

REVIEWING VOCABULARY

The following sentences are based on the story. Decide which of the words following the sentences best fits each blank. Write your answers on a separate sheet of paper.

1. Beth Perkins began her month-long _____ on her twenty-first birthday.
2. Along the way, she had to replace her _____.
3. Even though she was usually _____, Beth felt nervous about speaking in public.
4. She spoke about the _____ of her cancer.
5. She hated it when people would _____ at her.
6. Everyone's hard work _____ a major flood.
7. When she recognized her new _____, Beth waved.

Words: *averted, comrades, gawk, intrepid, prosthesis, remission, trek*

THINKING CRITICALLY

1. What do you think Beth learned about herself from her experience at St. Charles? What did she learn about other people and their attitudes toward those with disabilities?
2. Does the title of the story describe Beth accurately? Explain why you think so.
3. Have you or has anyone you know broken an arm or leg? What was it like not to be able to use the arm or leg? Discuss this with other classmates.
4. Think about a routine working day for someone who is blind. What must he or she do to get the work done?